Physical and Emotional; Relationshi

In Part III, to help you incorporate the
focus on action steps: 23 activities tc
outlined in Part II.

Editorial note: to avoid cumbersome he   and the like, whenever the gender can be either masculine or feminine, I will arbitrarily chose the feminine. This book can be one place for reversed gender bias.

PART I

Mindset

In this first part, you will be invited to walk with me through the garden that contains the wonderful mindset necessary to achieve your goals. Part II will take you deep into the four areas that are important for improving your well-being. Part III will show you a variety of activities that can make a huge difference in your daily life.

Part I is all about Motivation. Chapter 2 is about Commitment. Chapter 3 is about Beliefs. Chapter 4 is about Perseverance. Chapter 5 is all about creating your future.

Every journey, regardless of how long, starts with one step.

– Lao Tzu

"Dare to live your life as you dreamed.".
Move forward and make your dreams a reality.

– Ralph Waldo Emerson

Later on in the book I will ask you to make some notes. You can also download a companion PDF Activity Booklet by going to

http://www.soniaweyers.com/en/free-download

You can also use a notebook. You can also use a notebook to document your journey through this book.

CHAPTER 1

Finding Motivation

Why?

Ask yourself "Why?" What is it that you are looking for in a journey? Why did you choose this book?

Motivation starts with a reason. You must have a reason to change your behavior or start a new habit. Are you unhappy with something in your life? Is there a problem? Do you have a goal? Do you have a dream? What do you want to have that you don't yet have?

Consider this: When is the last time you did something without a reason for it?

You can have many reasons. Consider how you spend your day, and your week. Most people get up in the morning, go to work, school, or another activity. You also do chores such as grocery shopping or laundry. These are the things that many of us consider to be obligations. These are what we do because we must.

You might be able to see the motivation behind these obligations. So that I can wear clean clothes, I wash my laundry. I shop for food because it is what I need. I work to make a living and have the opportunity to do what I want. Even if you think you must do certain things, I encourage you to consider the things that you choose to do.

Now, take a moment to reflect on something you choose to do and why.

Feel how the "why" motivates you to perform the behavior.

Take some time to think about why you are reading this book. You probably want to live a happier life.

What?

> "Knowing your goals is the
> first step to achieving them."
>
> – Louise Hart

The second is to ask yourself "What"? What are you looking forward to from this book? What's your goal? What is your goal? Let's take a moment to explore that. What are you looking to do differently in your life?

Perhaps you feel bored with your life and want to find excitement. It is possible to wish for less sadness and anger. Even though you're surrounded by people, it is possible to feel isolated. Which is your reason for reading this book specifically?

Why Now?

In determining your motivation, you should ask yourself "Why now?" What is it that prompted you to get this book? Did you have a long-lasting feeling or an event that led to your quest for greater well-being? Take a moment to think about this.

I am grateful that you took this step, and that you are taking control of your health. I also invite you to take time to appreciate yourself.

You may be interested in seeing how much your life can improve if you follow the advice I provide throughout this book. If you are in this situation, I recommend that you take Diener's Satisfaction with Life Scale, which will assess how satisfied your life is. Then, take it again about three months after you have implemented the changes suggested in this book. Martin Seligman also offers a test HERE.

What to Do?

Now you know why you are reading this book, and what you want to get from it. Now what? Even if you know exactly what you want, sometimes you feel lost because you don't know how to get it.

> "Insanity" is doing the same thing over and again expecting different results.
>
> – Albert Einstein

You must change your behavior if you wish to make a positive change in your life. It's that easy. Keep doing the same thing if you don't want to make any changes. You are reading this book, so I know you want to make some changes.

Let me tell you about my journey.

As a young adult, I felt very depressed and didn't know what to do. Surprisingly, I had everything I needed. I was a good student, didn't have any material strife and wasn't abused. I heard it often: "You have all you need to be happy." This is totally unhelpful when you're not happy.

It was even more difficult to decide what to do. I had everything and was unhappy so I started therapy. Thirty years later, I spent approximately half my time in therapy. I tried every method, every tool and every approach, and I can honestly say that I have found peace and fulfillment that I didn't know was possible thirty years ago.

I Lead You

Although this book does not offer therapy, I will guide you through deep reflections and activities that will help you make better choices, choose new behaviors and find the best way to achieve the results you desire.

It is important to emphasize that while you can read the book, you will only be able to see the results you desire if you make some changes in your life.

You will find suggestions throughout the pages. I can't guarantee that everything will work for everyone or that it will be easy. If you don't try something new, it will not change.

Doubts

You may be sceptical. It could be quite simple, but you may doubt it.

I'm simply asking for your help. This book presents a range of possibilities that have been proven to be reliable, some through scientific studies and others simply by their inexplicable timelessness. Everything I present to you has been tested by me.

<u>Request #1: First, I ask that you refrain from judging me until you've tried my suggestions. I ask that you keep me open-minded for the duration of this journey.</u>

Curiosity

Curiosity is the root of open-mindedness. Recall why you are reading this book. How would it feel to achieve the results you desire? What would happen if you tried new behaviors?

I encourage you to be curious. You should be curious about what you find; curious about the resources that you have within yourself; and curious about how your life might change.

Ever wondered what it would feel like to be like someone you've met? My goal is to help you transform your life and make you feel different.

The next chapter will discuss the fuel that can change your mind, which is commitment.

CHAPTER 2

Commitment

It is important that you do your best to understand yourself and to "work" for it. Please take the time to consider the question before I ask it.

Take a moment to look in the mirror and think. Let's start by asking you to consider what commitment looks like for you and what your habits are when it comes to commitment.

Are you averse to the idea of commitment? Are you willing to commit to something, but then go about your life as if nothing ever happened?

Do you take your commitments as seriously as anything? Are you willing to sacrifice everything in order to keep your promises?

Are you able to meet your commitments easily? A hard time?

Can you name a few examples where you have kept your commitments? Do you have at least two or three examples?

Think about how you kept them. Consider the different ways you persevered with your commitments, even when it was difficult.

Can you name a few instances where you failed to honor your promises? Can you recall what happened? Did there happen an incident? Or was it negligence?

It is hard to change your habits. It is difficult to change your habits. Habits are automatic ways of doing things. This chapter will help you become more aware of your relationship with commitment.

> "Most people fail not because
> they lack desire but because
> they are too afraid to fail."
>
> Because of lack of commitment."
>
> – Vince Lombardi

You have a valuable ally in willpower. This will help you keep your promises. Let's take a look at how willpower works.

How strong is your willpower? Is it possible to make yourself do things that you don't want to do right now, even though later you will regret not doing them. Are you unable to complete tasks that don't appeal in the moment?

Kelly McGonigal's The Willpower Instinct is a great book to read about willpower. This is a simplified version. The ingredients of willpower can be divided into five categories.

The physiology and meaning of commitment is first. If you can:

- sleep enough
- eat healthy
- exercise
- meditate

Ironically, these things are thought to require willpower, when in fact, they can support our willpower more than any other thing.

Can you recall a time you went out with too many people, had too much food, or too much sugar? You might have had a hard time sleeping the night before, and you may not have been able to get up in the morning to do your exercise routine or finish that project you've wanted to complete for several weeks.

Imagine, instead, that you just had a great evening and ate a lot of healthy food. You woke up excited to get out on the run and work towards your goals.

You should now be convinced that there is a physiology to willpower. This means you should focus your efforts on getting enough sleep, eating well, exercising, and meditation. These will all help you increase your willpower for anything else. I'll return to this in Part II.

To increase your willpower, the second thing you can to do is to be kind to you when you fail. Self-compassion is a key ingredient in willpower. Chapter 7 will cover self-compassion more in depth. For now, remember that it is easier to be kind to yourself when things go wrong.

Visualizing your future self is the third ingredient in willpower. This will help you see that your future self is linked to your present self and make it more important to care about what happens to them.

Fourth, you can use willpower to think about what you might fail. Planning how to recover is better than tracking your successes.

Numerous studies have shown that people who are constantly reminded of their successes and keep track of their progress are more likely to make mistakes. You need to consider what you might do wrong to avoid that. You can use defensive pessimism which is a strategic application of pessimism that helps you keep on track. Answer the following questions to understand how it works.

    i.   What is your goal?
    v.   Which outcome would you prefer? What actions will I take in order to achieve this goal? iv. Which is the greatest obstacle? Where and when is this likely to happen?

vi. How can I prevent this obstacle from happening?vii What can I do to help me get back to my goal if this obstacle occurs?The fifth element of willpower, or "surfing the urge," is the ability not to be tempted to abandon your goals. Surfing the urge can be described as holding your breath for a bit longer than is comfortable. Your ability to hold your breathe for 15 seconds is a sign of your ability to achieve your goals.

Let's summarize the willpower rules:

1. You can improve your willpower physiology by meditating, sleeping and exercising.
2. Be kind to yourself next time you experience a setback in your willpower.
3. Be friends with your future self and think about it in a way that feels real.
4. Plan your responses to your failures. When you're faced with temptation, surf the urgeThere are many things you can do that will help increase your willpower. The fact remains that you are the first person to whom you have to commit when you make a commitment to something. Your mind can arrange for things to go your way, even when it is not in your best interests.

It is helpful to have someone to hold you accountable. Someone who understands what you're trying to accomplish and can keep you accountable.

Now is the time to really think about what you want. What are you willing to do? What amount of time can you dedicate each day to your pursuit of well-being?

Think about that, please!

It is a long-term commitment so it is important to find out your motivation.

Then, you must think about how you can support your commitment to get the results. This book is not meant to be put on your shelf and ignored. It is intended to help you make positive, lasting changes in your life. However, you have to be determined to do something with it.

Request #2: Give yourself an opportunity.

The next chapter will discuss how beliefs can affect your outlook. You may be holding yourself back from more than you realize.

It is often helpful to work with others as you cultivate the mindset that will help you start your journey. Join the Facebook group, "Happiness Now!" A guided journey

You can join it by going to www.facebook.com. If you don't have one, you will need to create one. Next, search for "Happiness Now!" The Guided Journey. Once you have found the group, click on the request to join and I will gladly welcome you.

CHAPTER 3

Beliefs

To be more motivated and able to commit to your goals, you must examine your beliefs. This is not about your religious beliefs. It's about your beliefs about the world and people. These beliefs can be unconscious, or not fully conscious.

If no one in your family has been to college in several generations, it is possible to believe you don't have the right qualities to be a college student. You might even give up your dreams and aspirations.

If your family is full of academics, it's possible to believe academic success is in your genes. It is possible to not work hard because DNA-stuff comes naturally. This could lead you to believe that academic success is in your DNA.

"Your beliefs are your thoughts. Your
thoughts are your words."

Your words are your actions

Your habits are formed by your actions

Your values are your habits

Your values become your destiny."

— Mahatma Gandhi

This book is meant to make a difference in your life. First, ask yourself if you truly believe you can achieve this. Are you able to improve your life by changing your beliefs? Are you a believer like Mahatma Gandhi that your destiny is determined by your beliefs?

It might seem absurd to you if this is something that you've never considered. It took me a while to accept the fact that my beliefs could have an impact on my reality, and not vice versa. It all begins with a leap in faith. I am willing to wait if you aren't ready.

- Request #3: For the moment, suspend judgment.

You reviewed your goals for this book in Chapter 1. You are now invited to reconsider your beliefs. What beliefs support the positive changes you desire to see in your life? For a moment, think about this. It is strongly suggested that you add something like, "I have what I need to improve my quality life."

It may be easier to imagine someone who already has what your desire, if you're new to this exercise. What would they believe? Put yourself in the shoes and experiences of someone who has already made the positive changes in their lives.

Write down the beliefs that will support your life:

> "Thoughts become things...
> Choose the good ones!"
> – Mike Dooley

This is illustrated by Jim Carrey's story. Jim grew up in a poor household and, even though it seemed likely that his parents would continue to live in poverty, he always believed in his future.

Jim Carrey, a young struggling artist, tried to make it in Los Angeles in 1990. He drove his old, beat-up Toyota up a hill that night. He sat looking out over the city and dreaming about his future. As broke as he was, however, he wrote himself $10 million "for acting services rendered" and dated it for Thanksgiving 1995. The rest is history, as they say. Jim was enjoying incredible success, making as much as $20 million per film by 1995.

This may make you wonder if it's magic. It sure does feel like magic when you combine three ingredients:

1. Your purpose is to feel aligned with your deepest values and congruent. You are confident that you're on the right track.
2. Commitment: You are committed to your commitment and have set up a way that you will honor it.
3. You work hard to achieve your goals. The law of attraction is something you may have heard about. It doesn't say, "Sit on your couch and visualize your dreams, they will appear!" Instead, the law of attraction

encourages you to really think about what you want and to commit to it. Then, you can orient your life towards that goal. Then things will change.

If you are more scientifically-minded and find this a little hard to swallow, consider the cognitive biases studied by psychologists. Human brains are so overwhelmed with information that they use heuristics to make decision. This leads to biases. One such heuristic is to look for evidence that supports our current view about the world.

This is known as confirmation bias. It is when our beliefs contradict the reality that we find ourselves in. We have an unconscious tendency to acknowledge the views that are consistent with our existing beliefs, and dismiss or ignore those opinions.

If you believe the world is a bad place and there is no chance for improvement, then you will find plenty of media coverage about the many tragedies that are happening around the globe. If you believe that the world is full with opportunity, there are many inspiring stories about people who have made a difference in the lives of thousands or hundreds of people.

This law of attraction also works. Your beliefs will influence your attention and affect your life experience. Your expectations will influence how you behave. Your life experience will change, and you'll be able to see how your beliefs can have a profound impact on your life.

This is what I have seen in my own life. I believed that no one could love me. It was difficult. It was a belief that I held in every close relationship.

After a few decades of therapy and learning new ways to think and be, this issue is no more in my life. It was not easy and it wasn't fast. It would have been a lot easier if I had found some of these ideas earlier!

Affirmations are a good way to shift your beliefs. Affirmations can be short but powerful statements. These affirmations are a way to be in control of your thoughts. Research shows that around 80% of our thoughts, or the majority of our thoughts, are unconsciously generated. Your conscious positive thoughts are called affirmations.

Affirmations are a way to express what you want in your life. Affirmations are used to remind us of what we have committed to. We also read affirmations to help our subconscious hear them, and we incorporate them gradually into our beliefs. This will sustain and support our mindset.

For the moment, I suggest that you use affirmations that are consistent with the beliefs that you identified and that support your goals for this book.

At this point, pick two or three affirmations.

- Affirmation 1:
- Affirmation 2:
- Affirmation 3:

One of my affirmations says, "I commit that I will open myself up to receiving love that is needed." Remember that story about me believing no one could love us. I have resisted this belief and am working to change it.

When you read affirmations, it is important that you allow your imagination to make them feel true. It is completely absurd to read this affirmation and then hear a voice inside my head saying, "Yeah! Like that's going to happen!" When we discuss morning and evening routines, we will be back to affirmations in Part III.

After you've explored the effects of your beliefs on you life and begun to choose your beliefs consciously, perseverance is key to creating the life you desire.

CHAPTER 4

Perseverance

Even if you have the right motivation and are determined, even if you work hard to align your beliefs, sometimes it

can be difficult. You must persevere when things get tough!

You probably have a strategy to achieve your goal. You might feel exhausted and lack of energy, which can make it difficult to achieve your goal. There might be other things that are more interesting, urgent, compelling, or easier. The news on TV, the children's noises, or the ringing of the phone might distract you. If you don't prioritize your priorities properly, you are more vulnerable to all of that.

It's difficult to make changes and adopt new habits when discouragement strikes. I will help you to find ways to keep going. To be able to deal with these problems better, you need systems.

Let me start by stating something that is a bit counterintuitive. It links to a key insight from the Greek and Roman Stoic philosophers. Sometimes, the best way to deal with uncertainty in your future is not to look at the best-case scenario, but to consider the worst.

The Greek and Roman Stoic philosophers believed that if you fear a condition, you should attempt it. Seneca advised that if you are afraid of losing your wealth, Seneca would recommend that you live as though you were poor while constantly reminding yourself that this is what the fear is.

Defensive pessimism, although not quite as extreme, is one of the best ways you can avoid getting into trouble. I have detailed defensive pessimism here. Chapter 2. This is a great way to keep you from giving in.

To increase your chances of reaching goals, consider what could go wrong. Then, plan what you can do now to get you back on track. You must show self-compassion when you make mistakes. This is a key ingredient for perseverance.

Self-compassion will be discussed in the book, but I want you to be aware. Numerous scientific studies show that self-compassion is more effective than beating yourself up. It is important to keep your eyes on the prize and to be able to forgive yourself for any momentary mistakes.

It will also help you to stay on track if you hold others accountable. It is important to be committed to yourself. It is difficult to let go of a commitment when things get tough.

Therefore, I encourage you to find a friend, someone who is on the same journey as you, or on another, so you can both support each other. Tell people you are on this journey. You will be more accountable if you tell more people.

What are you going to need when things get tough? Think about what a kind, caring person can do to support you and motivate you to keep going.

Your needs:

Reach out to others and ask for help. You can find someone you trust in your community and let them know what you need. You may be surprised at the amount of support you receive.

To help you persevere, it is important to keep your 'Why' in mind. This will allow you to focus on your goals, your motivation, and your time. It might be enough to motivate you if you choose a 'why" that is important to you!

If you're not feeling overwhelmed or tempted to abandon your plan, the next set of tips might be enough to get you back on track.

Begin by choosing an activity that will improve your mood, such as laughing at a mirror or jumping jacks.

A power song is also a good idea. A song that inspires you to move, dance and get in motion. It can be downloaded to any device that you have handy so that you can enjoy it when you feel discouraged. It will motivate you if you choose it carefully.

Second, you should start small. For five minutes, set a timer. For five minutes, do the behavior you wish to begin. You will likely want to continue once you start, but even if that happens, five minutes is still a lot more than nothing.

Finally, consider your role model and what they would do in your position.

Now you should have tried a lot of different methods to find perseverance. Which one is right for you? The next chapter will cover the elements of a Great Mindset. This will help you to explore your life improvement potential.

CHAPTER 5

Creating your Future

You have now examined your mindset one ingredient at time: finding motivation, committing to, identifying your beliefs and finding your way.

perseverance. They give you the ingredients of a great mind.

This mindset will help you to understand why you are here, clarify your beliefs, and give you tools to persevere when it gets hard.

Now you're ready to move on to Part II. This section explains the different areas that you can concentrate on to make things better. This book will help you become a better and more powerful version of yourself and live a wonderful life.

It is up to you to decide what that means for you. You can choose from a variety of options, and I'm certain that you will find something that improves your quality life.

I will guide you through the exploration of your physical, emotional, and spiritual health; your relationships with others in this world; your spirituality and meaning; and how you can connect with a greater sense of belonging.

Each area will be covered individually. Each area and sub-area will contain information. I may also invite you to try a particular behavior or reflect upon your deepest desires for your life. You will experiment with many things in each area to help you clarify your goals and live your best life.

Part II should give you a clearer idea of the area(s) that you wish to concentrate on. Part III will help you decide which actions you will take in order to improve your focus areas, which will increase your overall life experience.

It is important to actually try things. Reading personal development books does NOT develop people. You can only evolve by trying new behaviors and experiencing new things. While reading may change your outlook on the world, it won't make any difference if you don't take action. Your sense of possibility is expanded by experience.

After you've tried out a few new behaviors, you can decide which ones you want to keep. Then, you can put the skills that you've learned to continue doing the things that help you achieve your goals.

However, I recommend that you only try one thing at the time and not attempt to incorporate all of them into your daily life at once. You will never know what food caused the reaction and what foods you gave it.

You will get indigestion if you try to change your whole life at once. This will likely have one and one result: you'll quit trying to change everything at once. This is not why you're reading this book. So, take your time.

You can try the suggestions I made, and see how they feel. Then, you can decide if you want to incorporate them into your daily life. Next, you should be careful. Do not overdose on wellness, for Heaven's sake!

It is important to remember why you are reading Part II before you begin Part II. This is your ultimate motivation and your goal. Now, write down your goal. It is a good idea to keep this book close at hand.

Your Goal:

Your exploration will be easier if you have a clear goal in mind. You might find contemplative practices helpful in calming you down if you're too stressed. You might be more tired if you don't have enough sleep. You might want to change your eating habits if you feel that your diet isn't working.

Sometimes, you may be surprised at the results of small changes. I encourage you to be open to unexpected benefits from behavioral modifications. As we move through these areas, I encourage you to at least try one thing or at least five minutes. Be patient and take small steps, but be persistent in your explorations.

You will notice changes in your behavior as you incorporate new habits. Others might also notice the difference. It is rewarding to see someone else become inspired and begin to make positive changes in her life.

This book will help you use tools to cultivate better well-being regardless of your circumstances. It is almost certain that life will throw you curve balls. It turns out that feelings of sadness, anger, anxiety, and so on do not make any difference. This book will help you learn skills to manage life more easily, deal with difficult times more calmly, and take pleasure in the good times.

You may need to consult a specialist as I go through each area. To help you with your particular needs, you may need to consult a nutritionist or a sleep specialist. With that being said, I offer to you my scientifically-backed recommendations which have helped me and others along their journey.

PART II

Areas of Focus

You have already created the mindset to begin your journey to improving your life satisfaction. This second section will discuss the areas you should focus on to achieve greater peace, meaning, joy and quality of your life.

These areas can be described as your physical, emotional, and spiritual health. This section provides an overview of the four areas you should be concerned with.

Please take notes as you read this section. In Part III, I will discuss how to take action. You may also want to do your own research on the topics that are most important to you. Although I try to cover every aspect of the journey, each person's journey will be different.

Part II: Chapter 6 is about your physical health; Chapter 7 about your emotional health; Chapter 8 about relationships; and Chapter 9 about spirituality and meaning.

"Investing in knowledge pays the highest interest."

– Benjamin Franklin

"Knowledge is power.
Information is liberating.
In every society and in every family,
education is the foundation of progress."

– Kofi Annan

–
–

CHAPTER 6

Your Physical Health

"Keeping your body in good health is a sign of gratitude to the whole

cosmos: The trees, the clouds and everything.

– Thich Nhat Hanh

"When health is lacking, wisdom cannot be revealed, strength cannot fight, wealth cannot be accumulated."

intelligence cannot be applied."
– Herophilus

"Those who believe they don't have the time to exercise their bodies will soon find time for sickness."

– Edward Stanley

"The human body is sacred if it is sacred."

– Walt Whitman

"Health is the first wealth."

– Ralph Waldo Emerson

Nurturing Your Health

Your physical health is an essential part of any endeavor. It is possible to be in poor physical condition, regardless of whether you have a chronic illness, are out of shape, or struggle with weight, which will make it more difficult for you to do other things.

However, good health can open up new opportunities in your life if you put energy and resources into improving your health. This is all obvious. It is not obvious why so many people continue to make poor choices for their health, even though they are aware of this principle.

Some people blame a lack information, they don't know what to do. Others may feel it is due to a lack motivation or a lack of care. Others may still feel the same, but it could be due to a lack motivation or a lack of willpower.

Is it information that is keeping you from achieving great health? Information? Is it information? Do you think it is willpower? This question will help you make better choices in your quest for health.

As you read, I urge you to consider the many ways you can improve your physical health.

Since several years, I have been following a personal path to better my health. I have had great success. I'm almost 50 years old, have four children, and am in the best physical shape of my entire life.

I am confident that the strategies and research I did are working for me. I invite you to take a look at any parts you feel drawn to.

1: Food

Dr. Andrew Weil (www.drweil.com) and Isabel De Los Rios (www.beyonddiet.com) are my favorite sources of food advice.

If you don't know what you want, all the literature about food and marketing can be overwhelming. These are some principles I've come to believe from personal research.

- <u>What we eat is what determines how our bodies function and how efficiently it can provide nourishment for our cells. Take a look at what you eat over the course of a week, and ask yourself one question: Am I doing my best to care for my body? Start looking for ways to improve your health. Below are some suggestions.</u>

- <u>The bad thing about processed foods is that natural foods can be transformed with different chemicals to enhance flavor, color and appearance. This is not a good thing for nutrition.</u>Pre-prepared meals have higher fats and are not as healthy as the ones we eat. They also contain more salt and sugar.

Many commercial snacks are junk. Ever wonder how potato chips stack up so neatly? They aren't made with potato chips. The potato is simply an ingredient in the process that makes perfectly shaped chips look like fried potato pieces. As I tell my children, when it comes down to food, I advise them that:

Enjoy food that is as authentic as possible!

What does that mean? That means food that hasn't been subject to too many layers. Butter is not a problem simply because it is made from milk, but in a different format. You should eat as few ingredients as possible and make your own meals.

It's possible to say you don't have the time. While that may be true, being sick takes time. There are many ways to save time when it comes to food. It is possible to make large batches and freeze multiple meals. This allows you to make tomorrow's dinner and tonight's lunch simultaneously. Healthy eating doesn't have to take longer: almonds and apples can be eaten as a snack, rather than chips and snack bars.

- Reduce your intake of meat and eat more vegetables. The evidence regarding the health effects of meat is mixed and I won't take a position on it. The environmental impact of meat production is not under debate.

I have been trying to eat less meat for environmental reasons. I also started to eat meat from local sources. I avoid industrial meat. Vegetarians are becoming more popular and meat is becoming a much more controversial topic. While I caution you, I warn about the negative environmental effects of the meat industry.

Eating lots of fresh fruits, vegetables and healthy foods is better than eating junk food. This is obvious. It is important to avoid eating too many pesticides or other harmful chemicals. As much as possible, eat organic, fresh produce.

You might be able to purchase as much local as possible, such as farmer's markets and other short circuits. It may not be feasible or desirable for you, but it's worth considering.

A young European organization called "La Ruche Qui Dit Oui", which translates to "The Beehive That Says Yes", connects consumers and producers within a 250km/155mi radius of France via an online platform. Customers can also purchase a portion of a farm's production through Community Supported Agriculture. Personally, I prefer short circuits to organic food that has been flown half-way across the globe to reach me.

Local food does not necessarily mean you will have more options. For example, avocados and bananas are not grown in the northern European region. I believe that buying local food makes sense for health, environmental and social reasons.

This last recommendation is the one you should take from this chapter.

Reduce added sugar It is difficult to do this because sugar is found in around 80% of processed foods. Sugar is addictive because it increases blood flow to the same brain areas as heroin and cocaine.

You need to eliminate sugar-laden processed foods if you want to achieve good health. Sugar can be responsible for a number of diseases, including high cholesterol, clogged arterial, diabetes, metabolic syndrome and obesity.

We now know that cancer cells feed on glucose. As long as there is some fruit, our bodies don't need additional sugars.

You drink the first sugar you need to eliminate. Studies have shown that our bodies don't track calories from beverages as well as food. If you're used to drinking sugary beverages, this might be enough if your goal is to lose weight. You can drink water, herbal teas and teas as well as coffee. However, you should cut back on sugary drinks like sodas, fruit juices and most flavored coffee beverages.

What are the changes you feel you have to make in your food choices? Now is the time to examine how you eat food and what choices you make.

Take a moment to reflect on the following questions.

1. What is the content of the food I eat?
2. Do I eat a healthy diet?
3. What are three things I can do in the next week that will improve my health?2: Exercise

This section about exercise is based upon my 22-years of experience working out three days a week most weeks. I also have a natural curiosity that led me to research the health benefits of exercising while I was actually experiencing them.

It is important that you seek out personalized advice from professionals. At the very minimum, you should have a medical check-up to ensure you are healthy and that you can exercise as you wish.

At the gym that I went to, I was able to work with a coach. A typical session at the gym includes a 10-12 minute aerobic warm-up followed by approximately 10 exercises that target specific muscle groups or muscles. My program ends with a bench-pressing routine. My bench-pressing record stands at 65kg (143 lbs).

Exercise is the foundation of my balance. My experiences have taught me that exercise makes my life better. Let me share some information with you that may help you to be more self-motivated. I know that not everyone can do this.

1. Recent research suggests that inactivity can be worse than all other illnesses combined. Therefore, the recommendations for exercise are to move more throughout the day. Regular exercise does not seem to be enough to counter the effects of a sedentary lifestyle.Habits are key here. It will be easier to exercise regularly if you make it a routine. In Chapter 18, I'll talk more about habits.

    You will be more motivated to exercise if you choose something that you enjoy and take note of how it feels before and after. If you feel better after exercising, you will be more motivated to do so.

Both willpower and willpower have a reciprocal relationship. Although it may require willpower to exercise, regular exercise can increase your willpower. Exercise has a double advantage. Exercise is not only a great investment in your health, but it can also help you to be more determined to achieve your other goals.

2. There are many studies that show the benefits of exercising. Two main categories of exercise are:

   - Aerobic exercise like running and walking can increase your heart rate for a time.and

   - Strength training focuses on strengthening certain muscles.Each type of exercise has its own benefits.

   Aerobic exercise can improve heart health, increase metabolism and help with mild depression because it releases feel-good hormones.

   Strength training can have many benefits. It reduces osteoporosis risk and promotes autonomy. This is true not only in your prime years but also in your 30s, 40s, and 50s. Toned muscles can help in many areas of your life. It's as simple as helping to move someone or bringing groceries.

3. Regular exercise is an important part of weight management. According to the CDC in the USA, nearly 40% of Americans aged 20 or older are obese. 1 in 6 children is also affected by obesity. Europe has a slightly lower number of obese adults, with 10 to 30%. These numbers are unfortunately on the rise all over the world.Please take a moment to answer the following diagnostic questions:

1. Do I exercise at all right now?

2. If yes
    a. Do I exercise with enough frequency?
  b. Do I get a good balance of strength and aerobic exercise?3. If no
    a. How can I tell?
  b. Do you have any ideas for ways I can do a little exercise?3: Sleep

Sleep problems are becoming more common. You can skip the next section if you're one of the few people who are satisfied with your sleep quality and quantity.

If you're still reading, it is likely that your sleeping situation is not optimal. The complexity of sleep is multifaceted. This book is not meant to be a comprehensive guide. However, I invite you to take a look at your relationship with sleep in this section.

You might be like many others who are just slogging along on the crazy treadmill of life. It is possible to have difficulty falling asleep, or staying asleep; it is possible that you feel tired after a long night. Then there is the question of how much sleep is enough. Many people believe that sleep is a waste and are not able to ask the question.

This is simply false! This is supported by many studies.

Sleep deprivation can lower your sexual drive, age your skin, make you forgetful, affect your judgement, and be a threat to your health. It can also pose a danger if you don't get enough sleep. Numerous studies have shown that driving without sleep is as dangerous as driving drunk. Some studies indicate that sleep deprivation can make driving unsafe, while others show it can increase smoking.

If your sleep quality is poor, you should consider sleep apnea. This is a common disorder that causes you to have pauses in breathing and shallow breaths during sleep. This can disrupt your sleep and make you feel tired during the day. Sleep apnea patients are more at risk of being involved in car accidents, work-related accidents, or other health problems. It is crucial to seek treatment if you suffer from it.

Do you see the importance of both quality and quantity?

This section will help you understand your sleep needs and create the conditions for quality rest. Part III will help you decide what steps to take. If you are having more severe sleep problems, I recommend that you seek out specialist advice.

First, you need to understand that people have different sleep requirements. A few people are lucky enough to be able to function well on just a few hours sleep each night. Others need eight, nine or ten hours sleep every night to feel full and alert.

First, you must ask yourself: "How much sleep do I need?" I have a higher than average sleeping requirement and getting enough sleep consistently is my Achilles' heel. I am most happy when I sleep between eight and nine hours. This is why I get six to seven hours a day for a few days and then catch up on weekends. Sleep experts shudder at this. So, I'm right there with you!

Self-care is incomplete without sleep. You can determine how much sleep you get by not using an alarm clock. Then answer these questions to find out if you're getting enough:

- How many days a week do I wake up before my alarm goes off? How
- many days a week do I feel rested enough to go about my habitual activities comfortably?
- How many times per week do I reach for a stimulant, coffee for example, as a pick-me-up?
- How many times per week do I find myself snapping at someone or over-reacting in some way? Could it be that lack of sleep is the culprit?

What is your current perception of your sleep quality based on your answers to the above questions? Do you feel satisfied with the quality and quantity of your sleep? Or do you feel like there is more you can do to improve your sleeping conditions?

There are many things you can do to improve your sleep. The sleep doctors have many recommendations.

Exercise is a clear choice. Regular exercise is associated with fewer sleep problems. It's quite simple!

Meditation is another option. In the next section, I will discuss meditation in more detail. It has a positive effect on both quality and quantity of sleep.

You might find that your problem is difficulty falling asleep due to thoughts racing through your mind about the future. A quick tip is to grab a piece of paper and start writing it down. This allows you to let go of the thoughts and know that you will be able to access it again in the morning.

You will get more sleep if you create and maintain routines. A morning routine can set you up for a productive day, no matter what your night was like. An evening routine can also help you get to sleep well at night. You're likely to have heard that babies need a routine to help them sleep well. It shouldn't be any different for adults?

Your sleeping environment is also important. Experts recommend that your bedroom is used for sleep and sex. Your bedroom should not have a TV, computer or any other electronic devices. This is because it takes away work and obligations from your bedroom, and also because the light, sound, and pulse of electronic devices can be harmful to your sleep quality.

Comfortable bedding is essential for quality sleep. How comfortable do you feel your current bedding? If you answered below seven, I recommend that you invest in a better bed.

There are many rhythm-related recommendations that the sleep doctors can make. The sleep doctors recommend you keep a consistent sleep-wake cycle, limit your exposure to light in the morning and evening, limit caffeine, alcohol, and nicotine intake, and avoid waking up too early.

It is important to prioritize your sleep.

4: Cultivating Good Health

You can cultivate good physical health by taking time to evaluate your eating habits and researching the best eating plans.

This section encourages you to consider prevention. I will continue to share the strategies that worked for me, and encourage you find solutions that work for you!

<u>To take or not to take supplements?</u>
Supplements are hugely popular. They can help you sleep better, be more awake, have better digestion, or prevent these things from happening. There are many options.

Culturally, attitudes towards supplements can be quite sensitive. They can be very different from one place to another. Supplements are often equated with expensive urine. Some claim that you cannot get enough nutrition from modern food. Others claim that you don't need supplements if there is sufficient variety of high-quality foods. The answer lies in the individual. What works for you?

Personally, I found that taking a few vitamins and supplements helped me:

- B vitamins: I take B vitamins such as found in Brewer's yeast for example. This has helped me with some mild memory lapses I was having.
- Vitamin D: I live in Northern Europe where the whole population apparently suffers from a lack of Vitamin D because the sun is always lower here than closer to the equator. In addition, there is a lot of literature on how Vitamin D strengthens bones and immunity. So I take Vitamin D.
- Vitamin C: I also take Vitamin C regularly for its antioxidant and immunity-boosting properties.

For vitamins, I prefer to use natural forms over synthetic ones.

Body Weight

Although I've already mentioned weight loss in the exercise and food sections, I want to stress weight management as an preventative measure.

Obesity is a serious problem that is on the rise. It can increase the risk of developing type 2 diabetes and cardiovascular problems such as cancer.

Many overweight people can resolve their weight problems by changing to healthier eating habits and exercising regularly in a manner that suits them. Others may need medical attention.

A healthy weight management can have many benefits: less health problems, more endurance, and more self-confidence.

Alternative medicine

Allopathic medicine does not focus on prevention. It works like this: A patient with a medical problem sees a doctor who then gives her treatment and sends her home.

Although allopathic medicine has many advantages for our society, I am still on the quest to find a form that provides preventive medicine to keep my health good.

Although allopathic medicine is still available, I tend to use it less often. Progesterone was one of my premenopausal symptoms. However, it was causing me digestive problems. My doctor prescribed a treatment to relieve my symptoms. It didn't work. I had to find a better solution!

My path led me to a homeopathic doctor, who helped me find a homeopathic doctor. This homeopathic treatment actually regulates my hormones better than the progesterone. I don't suffer from the same digestive problems that I had six months ago when I began taking progesterone. It works for me much better.

Recently, I've also been using homeopathy to boost my immunity. Three winters back, I was struck with a severe cold. It quickly turned into a sinus infection. In a flash of determination, this time I decided to go natural. My homeopathic doctor had helped me shortly before I started this. I tried Echinacea, Grapefruit Seed Extract, Vitamin C, and other homeopathic remedies. Although my body was determined to fight the sinus infection, it took me two weeks to beat it. It also left me exhausted. Although I didn't realize it, I would be rewarded later for allowing my body to heal itself.

Homeopathy isn't the only alternative to medi-cine. There are many natural remedies that can be used to treat ailments, such as acupuncture and essential oils. These methods have good results without the side effects associated with traditional medication. Some even advocate that minor ailments be left alone and not being treated.

Your living environment's quality

Not only are our living spaces becoming more cluttered, but so is the amount of electronics in them. Mary Kondo's book, The life-changing magic and beauty of tidying up has many helpful tips. However, it is more difficult to reduce the negative impact of all our electronics.

The ever-growing number of electronic gadgets that we have is more pervasive than ever, whether it's your TV, radio, cell-phone, or Wi-Fi router. Although it is unclear if or how they may harm us, this is an area of research that I recommend.

There is a growing concern about the chemicals we inhale and what we are absorbing through our skin. This includes cosmetics and cleaning products. There are more natural options for cosmetics and cleaning products, which is a positive.

All of this being said, I suggest that you ensure you get plenty of fresh air and spend time in more natural settings, particularly if you live in an urban area. Consider all the simple steps you can take to improve your living environment.

Prioritizing your health.

Consider your health the greatest investment you can make in your life!

It is impossible to live your life in better health than in poor health. Good health, for example, gives you more energy and a positive outlook, which allows you to be more productive, rather than spending time in the hospital or going to the doctor.

I have done my own research. I recommend that you do your own research if you feel confident. Although there is a lot of information available, it can be difficult to know what to believe. I encourage you to trust in your instincts.

How I prioritize my health.

Let me close this section about YOUR health with a story about my health. I've always been in good health and consider myself fortunate.

However, I did have a lot of minor things. As I've said before, sinus infections were the most common thing that I experienced growing up. My allopathic doctor prescribed antibiotics to treat them. They do that for these infections.

As I mentioned in the section on alternative medicine I suffered from a sinus infection that I resolved to treat naturally three winters back. It wasn't easy, but I did it.

The flu struck me that winter. I experienced six days of fever and a stomach flu. They all were treated with the same basic premise. I am healthy and my body is resourceful!

My resolve to mobilize my body's resources strengthened with each passing day. I took sick leave when I got the flu and stayed in bed the rest of the time. I didn't take any medication, not for the fever, or the symptoms. Instead, I focused on resting, and hydrating.

My first day of being fever-free, it felt like I was in hibernation. I thought to my self, "I forgot how to enjoy all those days I was fever-free!" I also did the same when I got the stomach flu. I rested and tried not to get dehydrated. I then took probiotics until I could digest again.

I allowed my body to fight each illness, and strengthened it with a few supplements. Although I was unable to overcome the illness, I felt proud and capable. You may be wondering, "Why would she fight so hard when there are so many pills that make it easy?"

My answer is simple: It's been more than two years and I have only had a few days of the sniffles. At almost 50 years old, I feel stronger and more healthy than ever. My body seems to have learned to heal itself.

If you think I am a crazy person who rejects allopathic medicine, let me tell you that I did take anticoagulants last summer when I was diagnosed as Deep Vein Thrombosis. It wasn't something I liked, but it was what I did. However, after I had completed the allopathic treatment, I concentrated on healing and recovering naturally.

For resources, Dr Andrew Weil is my favorite and I also like the Sharecare platform. If you allow them, both will send you regular emails with the latest information about health-promoting behaviors in bite-sized pieces.

You may think that you are in perfect health and you don't care about it. You will understand the importance of good health if you've had to deal with health problems. Both cases are different and I recommend you make it a priority for your health to improve it. Treat it as your most valuable asset!

I mentioned I had two minor colds this year. It's amazing to me that they both happened the same day I was upset about something. Is it possible for our emotional and physical health to interfere? That is what I believe.

The next chapter will focus on your emotional health, and how it can be linked to your physical health.

CHAPTER 7

Your Emotional Health

"Those who can't weep with all their
heart don't know what it's like to
laugh."

–Golda Meir

"Science has learned a lot about emotions over the past decade.

Research has shown that your emotional awareness and ability to deal with emotions are more important than your intelligence.

Success and happiness in every walk of life, even family relationships.

— John Gottman, Ph.D.

Mahatma Gandhi said, "Happiness is when your thoughts, words, and actions are in harmony."

Emotions and Feelings.

Feeling them!

Motions: If there was ever a field worthy of attention, this would it! Many

Emotions are not compatible with work or family life in any way. Stereotypes such as "boys don't cry" are a common belief.

Or "Crying is a sign weakness."

It is common for me to see someone cry when someone is trying to stop them. It's almost as if the entire world is afraid of emotions. People pay professionals such as me to cry in the privacy of therapy sessions.

Your emotions are your own language, and it is better to listen to them than to suppress them. It is another matter altogether, and I will discuss that later.

Let me first clarify a common misconception. Positive emotions include joy, happiness, contentment, and cheerfulness. Negative emotions can include sadness, anger or fear. It is easy to misunderstand the meaning of the words "positive" and "negative".

It's easy to fall into the trap of thinking that positive emotions are "good" and that negative emotions are "bad." If yes, I will try to convince you otherwise.

Emotions are part of life. They show that you are affected and affected by the events in your life. Emotions are an important part of your internal information system. It is like denying a part or yourself the ability to express its emotions. It is the act of disowning that is dangerous.

This is why I recommend a different approach. Although positive emotions can be more pleasant than negative emotions, they all come from the same source. Blocking out negative emotions can make it difficult to feel any emotion. This is an unhealthy way to live and prevents you blossoming.

- Request #4: Perform the exercises as they arise. Don't postpone!

Exercise: Please spend 20-30 minutes doing the following exercise. Take a look at

Each of the following emotions can be experienced in a different setting. Allow yourself to imagine a situation that makes you feel that emotion. Then, take a few minutes to notice how that emotion manifests in your body. It may be helpful to make a list of each emotion in your activity book.

1. Joy

2. Anger

3. Sadness

4. Fear

5. Cheerfulness

6. Contentment

***

As I can imagine, you've experienced both the relative pleasure and discomfort of these emotions. I invite you to list them. Please remember that positive emotions are only pleasant emotions and that negative emotions can be unpleasant or less pleasant. That's all.

The link between our emotions and our immune system

Robert Adler, a psychologist, was the first to realize that emotions are sensitive to the immune system of the human body. We now know that emotions and physical health are interconnected thanks to his research. This link has been a part of my life, as I mentioned. Do you have this link in your life?

Uncontrolled stress and other negative emotions can weaken our immune system, which is one of the most important links. This holds true for many ailments, including the common cold and heart attacks. The risk of developing cardiovascular disease from recurring "negative" emotions is similar to that from high cholesterol or smoking.

Research has shown that anxiety is a key factor in illness and recovery. It is not the emotion you feel but how you handle them that matters. There are ways you can manage stress and anxiety. For this reason, mindfulness has been a hugely popular practice.

Mindfulness for dummies: here, now, and without judgment

> "Yesterday is history, tomorrow is mystery." We call today the present because it is a gift.
>
> – Bill Keane

When you feel an emotion, or any emotion at all, it is best to just be there in the moment. To become more aware of how it feels in your body and to observe it.

This part is likely to be familiar if you've already practiced mindfulness. But if not, it's a reminder to be mindful of your self and be kind to yourself.

You can cultivate mindfulness by setting aside a daily time to observe your breath and then returning to your breath whenever your mind wanders.

Mindfulness has become a popular buzzword. This can lead to them losing their true meaning. Let's take a moment to look at some of the different attitudes you can adopt to help with your difficult inner states.

Kindness towards yourself and unconditional friendliness are the first qualities you can cultivate. Although it's easy to say, it can be difficult to practice. However, it's the best way to overcome your negative inner states.

Two things can happen simultaneously when you feel difficult emotions: Your brain begins to look for elements that confirm this state of being true, and you stop feeling what you are experiencing.

A kind and mindful presence towards what is already there is the best attitude you can bring to these times. Being present to your internal states is a practice that allows you to be present and not escape towards what you want.

A BBC Family and Education News piece about mindfulness in schools was done. The video went viral on Facebook. The video featured seven-year-olds and six-year-olds explaining what mindfulness is:

- "The whole point of mindfulness is where you calm down and relax."
- "Mindfulness is where we have to calm down after playtime and get back into learning, by using our senses and working together." "It
- makes me breathe out all of the things I had to worry about."
- "You think deeply about your thoughts."
-
> "Alternatively, I wouldn't be excited and would not be able do my job."

Jon Kabat Zinn, founder of Mindfulness-Based Stress Reduction (MBSR), lists the characteristics of a mindful presence. These qualities are what he calls "the soil" in which to cultivate your ability to calm the mind, and see clearlyer.

Non-Judging means connecting with the impartial, honest, but kind, witness within each of us. People make judgments about their feelings and experiences, almost like a routine. Try to observe with impartiality how you judge others, if it happens. Try not to judge those you are judging.

Patience is the ability to see that all things happen in their own time. It is also a form wisdom. Try to be in touch with your impatience, and start with what is already there, rather than what you wish was. Notice when you feel impatient with someone else or yourself. Try to bring curiosity and not judgment to your impatience.

A Beginner's Mind is a way to bring an understanding to a situation. It's about remembering that you have never been there and now before. Every moment is unique. It doesn't matter if you have experienced a similar experience in the past. Try to bring newness to all the encounters you have with people close to you, such as family or friends.

Self-reliance is a prerequisite for trust. Trust comes from self-reliance and paying attention to your body. Your intimate relationship with your inner states will provide the best solution to any situation.

As they are both closely related, Acknowledging as well as Letting Go can be combined. This attitude will allow you to see the world as it is, and not as you wish them to be. You can still take action later to fix what isn't working for you, but this doesn't mean you won't. The first step is to recognize what is and to let your inner state be. This is important because it helps you avoid getting involved in blaming others or yourself. Before you decide what to do, it is important to clearly see what is going on.

This is the key idea behind "cultivate". These attitudes can't be acquired overnight. You need to keep cultivating them, especially when a certain attitude isn't present. It is possible to notice impatience or a focus on what you want rather than what is. To cultivate a positive attitude, it may be necessary to get to know your opposite.

Mindfulness can be developed by taking small breaks throughout the day and focusing on your breath for a few minutes. You can observe what happens, without looking for any particular thing. You will notice that your body is on autopilot. Take a deep breath, and you'll be able to wake up, even if it's only for a second.

Difficult Emotions

You have emotions and feelings. Some are more comfortable than other. I want to stress that even if you are happy and fulfilled, there is a place for difficult emotions.

You can develop a set mentality to help you get through difficult times in your life, as you have seen in the section on mindfulness. There is no magical way to eliminate all unpleasant emotions.

If you truly feel a feeling, it is possible to open the faucet of all your emotions. Conversely, if you resist a feeling you will clog the faucet. You must be able to communicate with your emotions before you can react to them.

Breathing

Sometimes, you don't want that intimate relationship. Sometimes, you don't have enough time, such as before you go on stage, during an exam or performance evaluation. Sometimes you just need to get some relief.

Your emotions are directly related to your breathing. Your breathing speed increases when you're stressed. Relaxation slows down your breathing to its natural rhythm. Your emotional life can have an impact on your breathing. You can replace an antistress pill by focusing on your breath. It may seem difficult to figure out how to do this.

Meet your diaphragm!

Are you able to locate your diaphragm? Locate your diaphragm at the lowest point of your sternum. Place your thumb below it. Did you find it? Keep your thumb there.

Now, I ask you to take three deep inhalations while your thumb is on your diaphragm. Inhale and push your thumb against your diaphragm. Exhale to feel your thumb drop back. This is how to take three deep, slow breaths. You will feel calmer if you really find your diaphragm.

Caroline Goyder has a Ted Talk on this topic called The surprising secret of speaking confidently by Caroline Goyder. It is worth watching.

Deep breathing can be a powerful tool. However, deep breathing can be difficult when you are most in need. It is more physiologically difficult to breathe deeply when you are stressed. Your heart rate and breathing speed will increase, making it harder for you to relax.

It is best to practice it when it is the most difficult. You can learn a lot about discipline and you will be able to take three deep breaths with your thumb on the diaphragm when your internal state is bothering you. You might be convinced to try it.

Learn to love your emotions

I hope you now realize that your negative emotions are not an enemy to be overcome, but a sign of something that deserves your attention.

You can accept all your inner states and make decisions that are in alignment with your core self when you do this. This is something that some people do naturally, while others need to put in a lot of effort.

Do not be afraid to take the first steps in discovering what works for your needs. This is a journey that will stretch you and allow you to see more. When you can feel and experience an emotion, and then go through it with awareness, you'll be transformed. This journey has been a part of my life for over three decades. The benefits are greater than I can express with words.

It is important to learn to recognize difficult emotions and allow them to live in a way that allows you to be intimate with them. Learning to cultivate positive emotions is another part of this journey. This will allow you to feel more satisfied with both positive and negative emotions.

The Science of Happiness

> My mom taught me happiness when I was five years old. They asked me my dreams for the future when I was a teenager.
>
> I wrote down 'happy.'
> They said I didn't understand the assignment, and I replied that I did not understand life.
>
> – John Lennon

Positive psychology has seen a tremendous growth since the mid 1990's. Before I get into the lessons that you can learn, let me first explain what positive psychology isn't.

Long time I believed positive psychology was a superficial recommendation. It suggested that if one tries to see the half-full glass, it will make you happier. This was not what I wanted, and it probably wasn't for many other people.

Although the field is now public, I still come across people who believe in the same belief system as the one I mentioned above. This is not positive psychology.

The field of psychology was traditionally concerned with psychopathology. This included negative emotions and their consequences, as well as helpful responses. Positive psychology uses research methods to identify positive behaviors and strategies.

You can find a lot of literature on the topics that I have covered, as well as many sources to help you get a deeper understanding of any of them. This section is designed to help those new to the topic and remind those who are familiar with it.

Positive psychology is a field that has exploded with scientific research. It offers many ways to feel more positive emotions, and handle difficult emotions more effectively.

Five of these strategies will be described.

Coping

It seems inevitable that life will continue to throw all kinds of things at you, some quite difficult, some downright painful.

The type of happiness I seek and encourage you to pursue is one that is compatible in your real life, not an idealized version. It is important to understand how to deal with difficult situations. This can be done with a few skills.

Breath meditation can help you relax. Take a minute to concentrate on deep breathing. The diaphragm can be used from the previous section. This can be done anywhere, anytime.

What if you could just take a moment right now, right there? Take a minute to breathe?

You can also regulate your feelings, although it may not come naturally. If you've never heard of this concept before, it may seem unbelievable or absurd.

First, notice that your thoughts can have a huge impact on how you feel. This is something you can see for yourself. You have actually already done it when you mentioned 6 emotions earlier in the chapter. Let's now confirm.

Think of any of the recent tragic events in many countries. Think of terrorist attacks as an example. You think about the orphaned children, broken families and the state of humanity that encourages people to commit barbaric acts. How does it make you feel to live in a country that is engaged in war activities? I feel most often sad and afraid about it. It's not uncommon for people to feel angry at this. Do you feel it? Are you noticing that these thoughts don't trigger happy emotions but the opposite?

Now, I want you to focus your attention on something you look forward too. This could be a vacation, a happy occasion, or just alone time. Think of something you are looking forward to and visualize it as vividly as possible. These thoughts can be cultivated for a few minutes.

***

Can you imagine how different it would be to think about a terrible event and think about something that you are looking forward to? This shows that you can control your thoughts and be more in control of your emotions.

You can learn skills to regulate your emotions. You can feel empowered to believe that your happiness is yours!

As I mentioned above, this idea may seem new to you. It would have saved me so much misery. This is the path that I chose to follow, and it has made a huge difference in my life.

"The mind can make hell out of hell, and heaven out of hell."

– John Milton

It is difficult to change your mind because, for evolutionary reasons our brains gravitate towards negative events.

- The bad news is it will take focus, time, and patience. The
- good news, though, is that practice does help.

These four tips will help you manage your thoughts so that you can manage your emotions:

1. Situation selection

    Avoid situations that can cause negative emotions and thoughts. You can avoid horror movies if they make it difficult to fall asleep or you have other sleep issues.

Although it may seem obvious, many people continue doing the same thing, believing that the results might change. My biggest problem is going to bed at night. I feel terrible if I don't get enough sleep. Do you have any such examples in your own life?

These three tips can be used when you are already feeling negative emotions.

2. <u>Labeling your emotions</u>

   This second tip is simple. The second tip is very simple. Simply telling yourself you feel angry, sad, anxious, guilty, jealous or whatever lowers the intensity. It is enough to identify the emotion that you are feeling.

   If you're stuck in traffic and it is bothering you, you might try saying, "Hmmmm, this frustrates me." This won't make the situation go away completely, but it may help to reduce the irritation.

3. <u>Attention deployment</u>

   This is a way to turn your attention away negative thoughts or towards positive thoughts.

   This is what you did! The terrorists didn't disappear just because you thought about your next vacation. It did make you feel better.

The last tip is called

4. <u>Cognitive reappraisal</u>

   This is a type of reinterpretation and is often linked to gratitude. Cognitive reappraisal involves looking at all aspects of a situation.

   If you feel anxious about a work-related meeting it may be helpful to reflect on how grateful you are that you have a roof over you head and food in your fridge. These items may not directly relate to the meeting but if you think positively about your job and reframe your thinking, it will help you see the meeting in a different way.

   It is also very important not to take certain things for granted!

Mindfulness meditation

When I was discussing emotions and feelings, mindfulness was a topic that I had previously discussed. Meditation is a topic that can be explored in depth by many people.

Mindfulness meditation requires that you observe the world around you with intense focus and in a nonjudgmental manner. You can start practicing mindfulness meditation by setting aside some time to concentrate on your breath. If your attention wanders, which it will, simply bring your attention back to your breath.

Let me start by addressing some common concerns and clearing up some misconceptions people have about mindfulness.

You may think:	When in fact:
- It means having no thoughts.	- Mindfulness is about changing your relationship to your thoughts.
- You need to understand it first.	- It is not something you can comprehend with your cognitive mind first; you really have to dive in.
- It will take months or years to see results.	- As little as five minutes a day for five weeks gives measurable results.
You may be concerned with:	A helpful response might be:
- Finding time, space, and availability for regular practice.	- Start with really short periods of practice, one or two minutes a day.
- Setting high expectations.	- Each mindfulness session is new, you have never been here and now before. Hence there is no bad session.

Regular meditation can bring many benefits, both psychologically and physically. These benefits may motivate you to meditate more often:

PHYSICAL BENEFITS:	PSYCHOLOGICAL BENEFITS:
- changes the physiological structure of your brain	- lowers stress
- reduces the expression of genes that cause inflammation	- improves sense of well-being

- lowers stress in stressful situations	- increases engagement in the present
- improves heart health (blood pressure, arrhythmia...)	- promotes kindness and compassion
- prevents the shortening of telomeres: it slows down aging and helps prevent the onset of disease – including cancer!	- increases chances of success
- accelerates the cure of psoriasis	- enhances creativity

Mindfulness can help you increase your success chances. What is the secret to your success? It increases your ability to respond, which in turn increases emotional intelligence.

This gives you a bit more time and space to decide how to respond to a situation. This allows you to have more access to your knowledge and experiences, which increases your creativity. It also increases your chances for success in other areas, such as your current quest to live a better lifestyle.

Gratitude

To feel more positive emotions, cultivate gratitude Robert Emmons is a world-renowned writer on gratitude. He defines it as:

> "A feeling of wonder, thankfulness, and appreciation for the world around you."

Research has shown that people feel happier when they have a positive attitude.

Let's try to conjure up gratitude. Find something you love about your life. Be specific. My exercise routine is something that I love.

Next, consider how it came about. Three days after I moved to a new place, I attended a gathering and two of the women there told me about a gym with a great personal trainer. That gym was my first and I continued to attend it for 22 years.

Think about who you may have to thank for this, or who was a part of it. My husband had moved me to this area to work, so the gathering was connected to his job. He played a part in my story. An older woman, whose husband was a friend of mine, took me to the gathering. She played a part. Two women told me about the gym, and I still exercise with one of them. The hostess also played a part in the success of the event. Because I get enormous benefits from my exercise regimen, I am grateful for all the people who helped me.

These items may be of relatively minor importance (e.g. "my coworker made the coffee today"), or they can be quite significant (e.g. "I got a big promotion". You might consider making this a part of your daily routine by keeping a gratitude journal.

David SteindlRast, a Benedictine monk, gives a Ted Talk about gratitude. He calls it gratefulness and not gratitude. It's worth 14 minutes!

He says that gratitude spontaneously manifests when two criteria are met: you have to be given something freely and the item is worth your time. To be grateful in every moment is the best way to access gratitude.

Every moment is yours to enjoy, and you can't get anything else if this moment passes. This is how grateful living begins. You are invited to view the entire talk.

There are many methods to help you live more gratefully. One way is to pay attention to the moment, while another is to reflect on the good things you have done in your day before going to bed. Many studies have shown that gratitude can increase happiness.

You can learn to be more aware of the good things in your life by allowing yourself to let go of the negative things. This may encourage you to be more attentive to the positive events in your life and to engage more fully in them, both in the moment and later when you can reminisce about and share these memories with others. It may be helpful to reflect on the causes of an event in order to find deeper sources of goodness and joy in your life.

People, when they're not trying to overcome an unpleasant past event, look forward to a better future. They think I will be happy when… Instead, I recommend that you concentrate on the little pleasures in life. This is the key ingredient to happiness.

You can savor what you are experiencing in this moment by taking the time to appreciate it. However, it is possible to also savor past positive experiences and to anticipate future positive events.

When you live mindfully, and take in every moment, you can savor the present. You can enjoy the moment whether you're with a friend for lunch or listening to music, reading this book, or watching Ted talks. It takes a lot of effort to change your mindset to positive experiences.

If you understand why it is important, it will motivate you. Why should you care? There are eight ways gratitude can increase happiness:

1. Gratitude encourages you to enjoy and take satisfaction from your life.
2. Expressing gratitude can boost self-worth, self-esteem, and self-worth.
3. Gratitude can help you deal with trauma and stress by helping you to reinterpret negative or stressful life experiences, and/or by decreasing the frequency of traumatic memories and their intensity. It can be difficult to feel grateful during times of hardship. However, it is possible to find the most value in expressing gratitude in these situations.
4. Recognizing others' help is a sign of gratitude. It encourages them to be more helpful and less materialistic.
5. Gratitude helps build social bonds and strengthen relationships. Grateful, positive people are more likely to be liked by others and to make friends.
6. You are less likely to be interested in the Joneses' activities if you feel grateful. This makes it less easy for you to compare yourself with others.
7. You can't be grateful and feel negative emotions at the same time!
8. Gratitude can counteract the effects hedonic adaption. Gratitude will help you maintain the happiness boost that positive events bring to your life. This is where caution is necessary: It is possible to live too long in the present, but I don't believe anyone in western countries, other than homeless people or Alzheimer patients, is in danger. It is vital to set goals and follow them. In Part III, we will return to your goals.

Let's say you are grateful for now?

Forgiveness

Evidence is abundant, from both academic research and personal development movements in general, that forgiveness can increase happiness.

It is not you who hurt someone if you hold a grudge against them. You will flood your body with negative chemicals if you keep a grudge against someone or feel wronged by them.

The person against whom you hold grudges isn't affected. You should not interact with the person you have a grudge against because they will be more likely to react defensively.

Forgiveness is the act of letting go or making amends to an offender. It doesn't have to mean that you must reconcile with them.

Research shows that forgiveness is a powerful tool for strengthening relationships, as well as reducing stress levels and anger. It can also boost happiness and optimism. Forgiveness reduces anger and resentment when they are not serving a constructive purpose.

This can help reduce stress by shifting your mental focus away from worrying about the past. Forgiveness encourages you not only to be kind but also to appreciate all the good things in your life. This will lead to healthier relationships and better physical health.

Forgiveness is a process that takes time. It should be started only when you are ready and have had the opportunity to grieve.

Forgiveness: I would like to close this section by quoting Nelson Mandela, who when Bill Clinton asked him how he could forgive his jailers, replied, "When I walked through the gate, it was clear that I knew that if they continued to hate me, I would still be in prison."

It is difficult to practice this stuff, I will admit. Our brains are wired for problems and to keep negative experiences more important than positive ones. It can be a difficult climb, but the view from the top can be breathtaking. You can trust me!

Self-compassion is the last topic in this chapter. It is far more effective than being harsh on yourself to help you achieve your goals. Let's get into this a little more.

Self-Compassion

> "With self-compassion we show ourselves the same kindnessess and care that we would give to a friend."
>
> – Dr. Kristin Neff

Kristen Neff, an associate professor of human developmental at the University of Texas, is a world expert on self-compassion.

Dr. Neff defines self-compassion as three distinct components:

1. Mindfulness is a state of awareness that allows us to be aware of what we experience and not ignore or exaggerate our problems.
2. Recognizing our shared humanity means that we can feel connected to others even when we are suffering.
3. Self-kindness is the ability to treat yourself with kindness and understanding, and not with harsh criticism or judgment.Self-esteem is a tool that motivates us. Unfortunately, self-esteem hinges on performance. Self-esteem can be paired with self-criticism.

Perhaps you've had the experience of thinking "I'm such a loser!" after you've failed at something important to you. This is a carrot-and-stick approach that can lead to fear-based motivation. I won't be OK if my failures are so I have to try harder and succeed to be OK.

You may be familiar with some of the effects.

1. It is possible to feel a bit depressed. This is not a good way to get motivated.
2. You might lose faith in yourself. You may lose your sense of competence if you continue to criticize yourself. Research shows that perceptions of competence are key to motivation.
3. It is possible to become so scared of failing that you give up on trying. Failure would have such devastating consequences that it is worth not trying.
4. This gives you the illusion of control. It seems that you can't fail if you say, "I shouldn't have failed!" I would succeed if I did everything right.Self-compassion differs from self-esteem in that we don't have to be better than others or achieve extraordinary goals. Selfcompassion picks up exactly where self-esteem can let us down.

Self-compassion is most effective when things go wrong. If you don't have self-compassion, you may think that if something goes wrong you're a loser. With self-compassion you can see the benefit in thinking, "Everybody makes mistakes now and again," and "In long-term, it doesn't really matter."

Self-compassionate people can accept themselves no matter how much praise they get from others. Positive reinforcements are the only way to boost self-esteem.

- Yet, a lot of people are afraid of compassion. One reason for this is that they strongly believe that they need their self-criticism to motivate themselves and keep themselves in line; and the Western culture supports that.
- Ask yourself right now: how is self-criticism working for you?

Self-compassion motivates you to want health and well-being and encourages and supports yourself towards those goals. Self-esteem tries to motivate by saying I'm not worth it if I fail.

Research has shown that self-compassion can be a powerful motivator. Three factors are key to this.

1. Self-compassion is about self-acceptance and not self-improvement.Self-compassion allows you to accept yourself, with all your flaws and all. Self-compassion does not involve self-improvement, evaluation or accepting yourself as you are.

2. The paradoxical theory that change is possible. "The paradox of self-acceptance is that I can change if I accept myself as it is."

– Carl Rogers

It is possible to wonder if self acceptance could be interpreted as being passive or complacent. Accepting things as they are may not motivate you to make changes?

As it turns out, when you accept your true self and embrace who you really are, you can see clearly what you have created. You will then care about yourself, and you won't allow yourself to suffer. Self-compassion allows you to know that even if you fail, it's okay.

3. Self-compassion is an emotional support system that allows for growth and change. Self-compassion is a great motivator because it allows you to tell yourself that you want to be happier and more fulfilled and that you will take care of yourself no matter what. You also know that you cannot control everything and will do your best to make it work.

Dr. Neff's extensive evidence supports the clear benefits of selfcompassion over criticism in a variety of areas, including parenting, weight loss, and goal setting.

Do you think you can treat yourself as a friend?

***

You have now learned strategies to cultivate positive feelings and worked on your relationship within yourself. Now you can start working on your relationships with other people, which is the topic for the next chapter.

CHAPTER 8

Relationships

"Let's be thankful to people who make you happy. They are the charming gardeners that make your soul blossom."

Marcel Proust - We all intuitively know that we are social creatures. Loneliness hurts, and human contact feels good. This chapter will encourage you to read a

Take a closer look at these words. What does it actually mean to be social?

Evolutionarily Social

Harry Harlow was a psychologist at the University of Wisconsin at Madison during the 1930s. He conducted research on monkeys. His seminal studies about the bond between mother and child in his monkey population are the most well-known parts of his work.

This discovery was completely unexpected at the time. Baby monkeys were placed in cages that contained two devices called "mothers". One was made from wire and could give milk upon demand. The other was made of cloth so the monkey could rest on it.

What time did the baby monkeys spend nursing over a 24-hour period?

They spent 1 hour of their 24 hours nursing, the rest was spent cuddling with the cloth mom.

Harry Harlow and his staff were stunned! They replied:

> "We were completely unprepared to discover that the comfort variable completely overshadowed and overshadowed all variables, even nursing."

Humans are like monkeys in that they have a deep need for love and care. When it isn't given or given in a way that suits us, it can cause psychological damage. In my therapy practice, I see a lot more of this.

Social connection is essential for our humanity. One experiment asked participants to name three wishes that they would like to receive from a Genie. In the overwhelming majority of cases, respondents wished for great relationships.

Brain imagery and other studies have shown that social rejection activates the brain's same circuits as physical pain!

Harvard Medical School runs the longest-running longitudinal study on adult development. It has been ongoing for more than 75 years. Let's find out what they have to say about this.

The Study of Adult Development at Harvard Medical School

Since the 1930's, 724 men were followed by successive Harvard research teams. They asked 724 men questions about their professional lives, personal lives, and health every year. Not knowing what would result. In November 2015 60 of the original 724 men were still alive and participating in the study. The study now includes more than 2000 children from the original 724 participants.

This group consisted of two cohorts. One was a cohort of Harvard sophomores, while the other was a cohort of inner-city youths from disadvantaged backgrounds who were not delinquent and grew up in Boston neighborhoods. Research teams used questionnaires, information from men's doctors, and sometimes personal interviews to gather information. The research teams gathered information about the men's mental and physical health, their career enjoyment, retirement experience and marital quality. The study sought to determine predictors for healthy aging.

Brain scans became more common as medical options improved. They also recorded them talking about their most pressing issues with their wives. They started talking to their children. They started to talk to their wives in the 2000's!

George Vaillant, principal investigator of the study, detailed the method and the results in three books. The Massachusetts General Hospital's Dr. Robert J. Waldinger is currently overseeing the study. They have collected thousands of pages of information on the lives and families of these men.

Robert Waldinger, current director of the study and a Ted Talk sensation, asks the following questions:

What have we learned from this? >>

Then he answers his own question:

He explains that there are three key lessons to be learned from the study, which aims to answer the question "What makes a life successful?".

1- The benefits of social relations are great for us, but loneliness is deadly. Socially connected people are happier, healthier and live longer.

It is unhealthy to be lonely. Unfortunately, many people suffer from it.

2- Quality not quantity.

It doesn't matter if you have many friends or are in a stable marriage. What matters is the quality of those relationships. This can have a negative impact on our health. Conflict is bad for your health.

The study included 80-year-olds who looked back at their health 30 years ago. Surprised to learn that their cholesterol did not predict their health the best 30 years later. Nope! It was their satisfaction with their close relationships.

People who had the most happy relationships at 50 were in the best shape for their health at 80!

> 3- Good relationships not only protect our bodies but also protect our brains. The 80-somethings who believed they could trust their partner retained their memories for longer. Even in conflict relationships, this holds true. Arguments are fine. The thing that really protects us, is the ability to rely on others, despite all arguments.

So, it is important to nurture your relationships, which are neither glamorous nor easy and that never ends, as they can have a positive impact on your well-being and physical health.

Vaillant's main conclusion states that "warmth in relationships throughout your life has the greatest positive effect on life satisfaction.":

"Happiness can be found in love. "Full stop."

Taking stock

It is important to assess how socially connected you are, given how vital social contact is for humans. You can take five minutes to reflect on your connection.

Here, quantity is not the goal. The quality of human connection and the depth of the shared experiences are what make the feeling of connectedness.

Allow yourself to feel right now how connected you feel. Let your intuition guide you. What level of connection and isolation do you feel?

Some people feel both. It is possible to have deep, satisfying friendships but feel distant from your partner or family. This can lead you to feeling isolated. You may also feel more connected to your family but less socially.

This is the time to take stock of your feelings of connection.

The next sections will cover different types of relationships.

Friends

Our social lives are one area where we can feel connected. This area is a subject that can appeal to many people. There are many types of people in this area. Some prefer one-on-1 interactions and intimate friendships. Others like to be with others and enjoy a more social life that includes parties, group dinners and outings. Different settings can offer different levels of intimacy.

What are your top qualities in a social life?

Groups of people are less likely to be open to sharing deep and intimate thoughts. Depending on your personality, and your personal history, this may be the best option.

Take a look at your social life. Are you as active as it should be? Are you looking for more social activities? Are you able to get together with your closest friends as often or less frequently as you'd like? Are you a fan of large groups or are you more inclined to socialize because you feel obliged?

How close are you to being able to have a socially active life? You should answer based on how your social life aligns to who you really are, not what others consider appropriate.

Although you may be active in social activities, you might find it difficult to make friends. You might be hesitant about emotional intimacy, or have difficulty finding people to share your feelings with.

Ask yourself how open you are to new friendships. Are they more casual? Do you feel more intimate with your friends? Are you comfortable sharing your personal information with friends?

As someone who is a huge fan of emotional intimacy, I prefer one-on-one and small group settings. My experience has shown me that sharing freely can be one of your greatest sources of feeling connected.

It is important to pay attention to how your friends and acquaintances relate to you over the next few days. See if there are ways you can make these relationships more enjoyable.

Family

Family is another area of connectedness. As Harper Lee tells Jem in "To Kill a Mocking Bird", this connection is not the same as it seems:

> "You can choose your friends, but you can't choose you family. An' they're still kin no matter what you do to them, and it makes your face look ridiculous when you don't acknowledge them."

Family is different than other types of relationships because they are still kin to each other, regardless of whether you acknowledge them. Family relationships can be passionate in many different ways.

A satisfying relationship with your family, who will always be your kin, can give you a sense security and connectedness. It also gives you the feeling of belonging to a lineage.

Family tension can lead to hardships and even tragedy. Recently, in France, a man killed his wife's brother, his entire family, and two of his young adult children over a sour inheritance!

Even if it doesn't go that far, it can cause strain in family relationships. It takes a lot to resist a bond that is irreparable, regardless of whether it is genetic or historical.

You might have relatives who are older depending on your age. Many of us feel very sad when our elders pass us. They are part of your past, no matter how close you have been to them. They are part of your DNA.

Many people feel more lost when they lose a loved one.

If you have elderly relatives that you are not able to get along with, I recommend you try to create peace. Use some of the tips in the emotional health chapter (Chapter 7), and you may be able spend more time with them to find some resolution.

Your family has a common history. It is the source of intergenerational transmission. You can decide if sharing some aspects of your past with them is desirable or possible.

Love

The best and worst in people can be brought out by love relationships. In fact, the closer we are to someone, the more intimate our relationship patterns and deepest wounds become.

We tend to select partners who can recreate a familiar emotional environment for us. This may be something we have done with mixed results. Sometimes, we are unable to resist falling madly in love with someone who makes us miserable. Sometimes, our lover is the exact opposite.

Early relationships left me believing that I could not be loved. This belief was something I didn't even know existed. This is how I saw my world. This was the effect of the section on beliefs. In retrospect, it became clear that I continued choosing relationships with people I didn't feel loved.

This belief was only exposed and changed after I had gone through significant personal growth. I have a wonderful relationship with a man that is far more than I could ever imagine.

Are there any ways that your love life reminds you of past experiences? Is your love relationship more supportive or less? No matter what your answer is, it's possible to improve your love relationship.

Elizabeth Gilbert, author of Committed, offers a useful metaphor for this. She cites her husband, the gem-buyer, in her book:

A parcel is a random assortment of gems that the miner... has put together. [...] It is possible to get a better deal by buying them all together in a group. But [... will try to sell you his poor gemstones by packing them with some really nice ones.

You can get a better deal if you ignore the good gemstones. You can put the good stones away, and then take a close look at the bad ones. Take a moment to look at them and ask yourself if you can work with them. What can I do with these?

The same goes for spouses. You may find your spouse has wonderful, positive qualities. However, your spouse might have some negative aspects that you don't like. How do you handle those things?

It is important to ask yourself "What do you want in a relationship?" Which type of person would best suit you? This question is not the same regardless of whether you're single or in a committed relationship.

It is possible to clarify your expectations of a relationship with someone you love, regardless of whether it is in the beginning or not. Clarifying expectations can help relationships reach the next level.

Breakdowns

Sometimes it may not be possible to reconcile differences. Sometimes a relationship can reach a breaking point.

It is crucial to find peace in your own heart. I urge you to forgive yourself and the other person if this is your situation. Your inability to connect often stems out of a limitation you don't know.

Sometimes it can seem impossible to connect with other people. You might try looking for new connections. Maybe inspiration is in the next chapter.

CHAPTER 8

Spirituality and Meaning

"Just like a candle can't burn without fire, so too can men live without a spiritual existence."

– Buddha

"The mysterious is the most beautiful thing that we can experience.". It is the source for all science and art."

– Albert Einstein

"It's not the length of your life, but the depth of your life.

– Ralph Waldo Emerson

"The journey inwards is
the longest."

– Dag Hammarskjold

"Most people live their lives as though they have another one."

– Ben Irwin

> "A little bit of us can be found in everyone we meet."
>
> – Stephen R. Covey

Spirituality Light

Even though I haven't been spiritual for a while, I decided to include a chapter about spirituality and meaning. I still feel my way. It is important to note that I'm not talking about religion. I respect all beliefs, as long as they are similar.

Organized religion is not a good way to experience spirituality. It has more to do than bringing together like-minded people. Thus, I'm not addressing religion but spirituality. I will give you an overview of how my spirituality-light approach contributes to my life.

If you are a veteran of spirituality, I suggest that you bring a beginner's mindset to this section and see if you can find anything new. You are welcome to join the spiritual journey if you are a beginner!

This chapter will share my thoughts, my reflections, and some of the beliefs that I hold.

As I do throughout this book, I invite you to be curious about your beliefs, and to see if my path resonates with you.

Inspiration

My spirituality is based on what inspires and motivates me. This is why I use the Middle English meaning of the verb inspire (v.). It also means "breathe or bring life or spirit into the body."

What would you say to the question "What for?" What beliefs do you have about why we're here and what our purpose?

Are you convinced that we are part in something larger? Are you a fan of Elon Musk's idea that we may be part a large simulation? Do you prefer to see us as free will and random events in the world without any particular purpose or meaning?

Personally, I've been thinking more about how we all are connected and how it is important to reflect that in my daily life. I am not sure if there is a greater purpose, and it is hard for me to imagine us as part of a simulation.

I find it helps me to find inspiration every day by remembering that thoughts can become things. This is something I encourage you to think about if you're not convinced.

You are more likely to have negative self-talk if you have a lot. It's easy to see this backwards, and think that people who are lucky have happy thoughts because of their luck.

You are invited to examine your thoughts and make changes to those that don't support the life you want.

It's possible that the universe has your back!

Beauty

There are many natural beauty on Planet Earth that may inspire you. This section invites you to think about awe, the feeling of wonder when confronted with natural beauty.

You may be able to access beautiful natural sites depending on where you live. Or you might travel to them on vacation. You may even have photos of these places on your computer.

No matter if you love the mountains, forests, or the sea, there is one thing that all of these places have in common: they are larger than us. If you're attentive, you can feel a sense of appreciation and recognition that you are in the presence of natural grandeur.

Research on the effects of feelings of awe on our well-being suggests that they can have an impact on our health.

Being in nature has many other benefits, besides the sense of awe (which I highly recommend you embrace), These benefits may be cognitive in nature, helping to sharpen thinking and creativity, or short-term memory. They can also be health-related, such stress reduction, immune system boosters and possible anticancer effects.

If you are like most people and don't have immediate access to beautiful natural places, you might be able to access a park or a small garden with just a few plants.

You are encouraged to spend five minutes with nature at your next opportunity. For five minutes, just be with nature and pay attention to what you feel.

***

What was it like? Are you feeling more connected?

The sky is a grand natural manifestation I know of. The sun rises and sets every day, and stars and planets can be seen at night depending on the amount of light pollution or cloud cover.

It is amazing to me how the sun and clouds interact in the sky, and the images it creates. It's a small part of my daily life that I appreciate. All it takes is to be attentive.

What do you see in the sky? Even in the middle of the night, there are still amazing things to see, that can give you a feeling of connection.

Self-Realization

Spiritual alignment is a part of self-realization, according to me. What does that mean? This does not mean one should be selfish or neglect one's needs. No.

This is how you can find your inner self and align with your spiritual path.

This is perhaps clearer if you think about purpose. Is this your life's purpose? My mission is to help people find their key to happiness and self-fulfillment. This is why I wrote this book.

My greatest wish is for you to read this book and take action to make your life more in line with your core values, your environment, and your heart.

It's possible that you already have an idea of your purpose. If not, you can open your activity book or get a piece paper and a pen. Set a timer for ten minute and begin writing "What I most want to accomplish in my lifetime is ..."" and then just write what comes to your mind. If you feel stuck or unable to find your way, you can write anything, including a shopping list, a letter for a friend, or anything else that might inspire you to start writing.

Keep in mind that your goal is to achieve what you want in this life. You can always take another set of ten and maybe even another. You will eventually find the elements that give meaning to your life and give you a sense if purpose.

Although this is one way to hear what I call the whisper inside, there are other ways. I'll be sharing with you a few actions that can help you get closer to your goals. To help you self-realize, I encourage you to consider the possibility that aligning with your inner truth is the best way to manifest in this life.

This inner truth can be hampered by your life experiences in the early years of your life. You are probably reading this book because you can relate to the struggle to hear your inner voice and searching for your true self.

It is difficult to see the path to self-realization. It is the result a process of discovery and self-discovery. You can think of yourself as an explorer. While you live your daily life, alongside the routines you have in place, your senses are constantly awakened to find out more about your next steps.

This is a personal path and it requires courage to walk the talk. This is about being yourself. It is possible to live in conflict with your inner truth in ways that are difficult to accept.

Sometimes, it takes courage and determination to face your fears. As you begin to live more in accord with yourself, you might feel inadequate. You may also experience loyalty conflicts between what you think you should do and who you are. This is a journey of personal growth.

This path may seem more advanced to you than others. It is a path that we all can follow and it is helpful to bring a beginner's perspective. Selfrealization is a never-ending journey. It is a life-journey.

This journey is like many others. It can bring you great rewards, but also great pain. It is important to keep your commitments in mind during these moments. Part I covered commitment and everything that comes with it. You can always go back to Part I if you are having trouble with your commitment.

Causes

Participating in a cause that you believe in is one way to reach self-realization. You will most likely feel a sense of purpose by engaging in activities related to the cause.

Are you involved in a cause you love? You take actions in support of a cause you believe is worthy. Engaging in small actions that benefit the environment is my favorite cause.

It is amazing to consider all the wonderful things that this planet has to offer and how much we take from it in the industrialized world. This not only affects the future opportunities for our children, but it also impacts large and already economically poor populations. You can see my point of view here

Leonardo Di Caprio's documentary Before the Flood

There are also more hopeful stories, and Tomorrow is one of them. Five everyday actions can be taken to ensure a better tomorrow:

1. Eat more organic food, less meat
2. Choose a supplier of renewable electricity
3. Local and independent sources of buying
4. Choose an environmentally responsible bank
5. Reduce, reuse, recycle, repair, and shareThese dimensions are very important to me in my daily life. I take small steps to reduce my use of fossil fuel energy and the amount of waste I produce. Every action that I take to support this cause brings me joy.

Which cause will bring you joy?

The Power of Now

One of the most effective ways to improve your spiritual path is to pay attention to the moment. In his book, The Amazing Ekhart Tolle

Power of Now: A Guide for Spiritual Enlightenment

> Time is not precious because it is an illusion. The only thing you can consider precious is the point beyond time.
>
> The Now. This is very precious indeed. The more you focus on this, the better.
>
> Time--past, future and now--the more that you lose the Now, the most precious gift there is.

You must focus more than the moment if you want your life to move forward, plan your future, and achieve your goals. This is obvious. In the western developed world, it seems that we either tend to be too forward-looking or stuck in the past. Learning to live in the moment is something that most people find worthwhile.

You can focus more on the present while you work towards your future-oriented goals and make peace with the past.

The act of being in the moment requires letting go. This is something that I have learned from both my own experiences and those of my clients. Many clients who are upset about the current state of things think that to let it go is to stop worrying about everything and just follow the flow. This is not what I mean.

There is a way things are in each moment. That is fixed in that moment. Your response to what is is what is fixed. This is where power lies: you have the power to be with what is, and AIM to move in a direction that supports your personal path.

While I am writing this, I am thinking about a client that I work with. She is extremely upset with the management of her organization. She claims that they don't do the right thing. This is not how you should manage.

She sees that this is a negative for the entire organization. This makes her very unhappy as she constantly wants things to be different. She must be able to discern what is and what she can do for others. It is frustrating to live in a state where you want things to be different than they are.

This frustration can be overcome by cultivating a sense of presence in the present moment. Mindfulness and breathing are two ways to get back into the present moment. Connecting to greater things is another simple way to reconnect to the present moment. Connecting with nature, for example, is another way to experience presence.

If you are struggling to accept the world around you, try looking outside. You will find many activities to help you cultivate presence in Part III.

Living Together

As part of my vision of a healthy spiritual existence, I consider some ways to live together essential.

In times like these, togetherness can be problematic on some levels. Recent events, such as the Brexit vote or the election of Donald Trump seem to show an increase in Us vs Them attitudes.

Since the Middle Ages, there have been no more barriers or walls in the world. These dividers are used to separate Us from Them. Research has shown that infrahumanization is a result of these separations. This term was created by Jacques-Philippe Leyens to denote a tacit belief that an in-group is more humane than an out-group which is less.

It may not be easy to live together when there are historical facts that make it easy for people to divide the population. To cultivate the ability of living together, it is important to examine your attitudes towards different people.

We are all different, but we all have similarities too. Our biggest similarity is that we are all human. The documentary by that same title exemplifies this fact beautifully!

However, there is an inclination in politicians and in people to highlight differences. Conflict can arise from racial and religious differences. It is possible to move beyond these differences and open up to new possibilities.

Recently, a beautiful Danish advertisement went viral on Facebook. It featured people standing in squares on the floor that were drawn by someone. This was according to standard categorizing.

The video features a group of Danes from different backgrounds who find that they share more in common than their exterior appearances suggest. It starts with "It's easy for people to be put in boxes: there are us and they. The highest earners and the ones just scraping by. We trust those we can trust, and we avoid those we don't. There are new Danes as well as those who have been there all along.

They ask participants to come forward with new labels: step-parents or people who have been bullied, bullied, or those who had sex in the last week. The 'boxes begin to disappear, and new groups emerge from shared experiences.

The video ends with a profound realization: Maybe there is more to bringing us together than what we think.

If you are focusing on the differences, I encourage you to look for one commonality.

Even though it can sometimes be hard, it is possible to still foster a spirit of tolerance. You might be able to grant another person the right of existence even if you don't feel the sameness.

Some people find it easier to tolerate differences because of their upbringing or life experiences. This is an opportunity to grow if you are averse to different cultures.

This also includes forgiveness. To overcome any obstacles to tolerance, it is better to cultivate forgiveness. Chapter 7 discussed forgiveness. It is not a good idea to hold onto grudges and wrongdoings. They make people less happy and less able connect with others.

I pose the following question: What kind of spirituality is possible if you are unable to live together as a worthwhile goal?

My personal answer: none!

Money

It may be surprising that you find money in a chapter about spirituality. Take a moment to listen and maybe you can join me in this endeavor.

Many a love-hate relationship revolves around money. It may have been this way for a long time, but it is more likely now than ever. It has never been a more prosperous planet, and the inequalities between people have never been greater.

It is not money, if you really think about it?

It's a tool for exchange. It serves two purposes. It standardizes value, which allows trading to be possible without the need to find someone to trade with. It stores values, which allows for saving for later spending.

Spirituality and money can meet when you understand that money is a symbol for human productivity and achievement. If people are passionate about what they do and earn a decent income, the money they get in return is a symbol of their achievement and productivity.

> "Money, without which you can't
> make decisions,"
>
> Complete use of the five other ones."
>
> – W. Somerset Maugham

This is a great opportunity to reflect on your relationship with money. Are you happy? Do you want more or are you satisfied with what you have? Are you averse to money or find it disgusting? Do you value earning it and appreciate the opportunities it gives you?

We often have a view of money that is shaped by our upbringing, as well as the realities of the society in which we live. Sometimes, what we see can make money look bad.

The scandals surrounding the 2017 French presidential election involve large amounts of money that were allegedly embezzled by people with more than enough. This makes money look evil. Rich people are guilty of tax avoidance, which is why money has characteristics like dishonesty or greed.

My suggestion is to remember that greed and money are different things, even though it can be quite ugly when they meet. You should both demonize and de-sacralise your money. Money is a tool to store and standardize value.

To help you develop spirituality and live a more fulfilled life, I suggest that you reflect on the connections between money and your purpose.

My professional activities align with my mission to help people find their keys to happiness and self-fulfillment. When I get paid for what I do, it makes me feel connected to the larger purpose I am working towards, and that makes me happy. Concerning how I spend the money, many of my decisions are rooted within my environmental engagement which is also joyous.

It can be difficult, but it is possible to earn your money in ways that align with your purpose or cause and are compatible with your spiritual involvement. If you use your money to build a life that reflects that purpose, I believe you have succeeded in de-sacralizing and un-demonizing money.

***

Part II focuses on several areas that can contribute to your well-being, connection and wellbeing. I covered Physical, Emotional, Relationships, Spirituality, Meaning, and Physical Health.

Part III will cover 23 activities that can be used in different areas of your daily life. Now is the time to get out there and do some things. You won't know how something works if you don't try it!

PART III

Getting into Action

"Nothing reduces anxiety quicker than action."

— Walter Anderson

"Up until a certain point, a man's world is shaped by his environment and his heredity. Then it becomes his responsibility to mold the clay of his existence into the kind of life he wants.

It is what he wants it to be. Everyone has the power to say, "This I am today, and this I will be tomorrow."

– Louis L'Amour

"The purpose and meaning of life is to live it."

– Clarence Darrow

"Do what you think is impossible."

– Eleanor Roosevelt

"Success can be attained by being the right person."

– Jim Rohn

Resilience is the ability learn from and grow from difficult situations. This is a strong character trait and one that I highly recommend to anyone. This third part, Getting Into Action, focuses on two types of activities. One that promotes peace and joy by promoting more positive or supportive emotions, and one that gives you the tools and tips to recover from difficulties. They promote resilience together.

CHAPTER 10

It's Time!

"A goal without an action plan is just a wish."

- Antoine De Saint-Exupery This is when you should start focusing your attention on specific actions, routines and healthy habits that will drive happiness. The perfect plan

The plan that is optimized for you can include many little things!

To enhance the reading experience, I have suggested that you do a range of activities throughout the book. This Part consists of all the activities I would like you to try.

These are activities, so reading about them is not enough!

You are encouraged to try all of them. I have included a Table in the Annexe where you can plan each activity and take notes after each one is done. Although I don't expect you to include all of these activities in your daily life, you will learn valuable information about your own preferences and what interests you. You will also discover what your priorities are.

You should also try different things. Sometimes, even though they may be uncomfortable, you can still reap the benefits of doing them again and again. It is a good rule of thumb to do a new activity seven times before you decide how you feel about it. According to the most recent research on habit formation, you must do something 60-six times before it becomes a habitual. This is to test it out.

It is a good idea to take time to think about what you want to accomplish and which areas of interest are most appealing to you before you start the activities.

It can be very helpful and even essential to clarify your goals before pursuing them. It is helpful to be specific if you are drawn to a chapter about Your Physical Health. Maybe you have problems with your sleep, such as not getting enough or sleeping well. Maybe something is wrong with the way you eat. Maybe it's your exercise habits that need to be improved. Perhaps it is the way you approach healing that you need to improve.

You might not have a specific health issue but are interested in improving your health. You may feel inspired to take on more responsibilities even if you don't have a clear pain point.

Are you unsure of what information you have or are you unable to make the right decisions? Do you need to do more research? Or do you need motivation to get started?

Just a few moments ago, I walked you through some possible areas of focus for your physical health. Now, I invite you to do so for all areas in Part II.

Part II, Areas of Focus, covered four broad topics.

1. Chapter 6 was about your physical health. You reflected on how food, exercise and sleep affect your health.

2. In Chapter 7, I talked about your emotional health. To see how different situations can lead to different emotions, you did an exercise. Also, you found your diaphragm by doing a 1-minute breath meditation.

3. You reflected on your relationships and how you feel connected in Chapter 8. Also, you thought about how you feel in friendships and what you want in a relationship.

4. In Chapter 9, I explored spirituality and meaning. You pondered the fundamental "What for?" question, and then reflected on your purpose or meaningful causes. You reflected on the relationship between money and beauty, and emphasized beauty and being present in the moment. You have done so much already.

This section of the book will help you take your skills to the next level. Ask yourself these questions for each chapter in Part II:

- "How satisfied am I with where I am in this area of my life?"

You may want to take notes in your activity booklet or your notebook or you may prefer to loosely muse on this question. My aim here is to orient your attention in the chapters that follow, towards the activities that will be most beneficial to you.

How satisfied are you with:

- Your Physical Health?

- Your Emotional Health?

- Your Relationships?

- Your Spirituality and Sense of Meaning?

At the same time as I invite you to think ahead of time about the areas of your life you wish to improve upon, I encourage you to approach each activity with an open mind.

In the next several chapters, I will describe a collection of routines and activities, and I invite you to make a note in Table 1 from the appendix or in your activity booklet and plan when you will try them. This will launch the building of your personal plan of action.

CHAPTER 11

Morning, Evening, and Sleep

Routines have the advantage that they become exactly that: routines. When they become habitual, you have a good thing going! As long as you have picked them wisely, of course. While I focus on morning and evening routines, you may have routines at other times, and that is great too.

Morning Routines

A lot of people engage in some sort of morning routine. Some read, some write, some meditate, some go running or work out; there are many possibilities. It is important to find a routine that works for you and that suits your needs.

First you must ask yourself what you are aiming for in a morning routine. If you have trouble waking up, you might be aiming to wake up more completely. In that case, some form of physical activity might be a good idea in order to get your blood flowing. If you have trouble focusing in the morning, you might aim to control your focus and thoughts. In that case, you might want to focus yourself with meditation or visualization.

If you find that you have already committed to certain activities but you can't fit them into your busy schedule, your aim might be to complete that activity in the morning. In that case, you need to schedule time for that activity whether it be read for half an hour, write for some amount of time, or exercise.

Personally, I like Hal Elrod's *Miracle Morning Routine* that covers all bases. You probably have heard of Hal's work but in case you haven't, let me summarize it here. The Miracle Morning Routine fits into the acronym SAVERS:

Silence (meditation)
Affirmations
Visualization
Exercise
Reading
Scribing (writing)

Hal gets up an hour earlier and does 10 minutes of each of these activities. Personally, knowing myself, I am a night owl, and getting up a full hour earlier is too much for me. So depending on what I have going on in the morning, I get up anywhere between 20 and 40 minutes earlier.

When I wake up later or need to start my day sooner, I do two minutes of the first four activities, six minutes of reading, and three minutes of writing, for a total of 17 minutes. When I have more time, or a later start, I like to do four minutes of everything and ten minutes of reading, which adds up to 30 minutes and takes 35 to 40 minutes with transitions.

Lisa Abramson and Vanessa Loder at "Mindfulness Based Achievement – the new MBA," include a morning routine in their success ritual. According to them, the way you start your day is essential to creating your success with ease.

In creating a morning routine, it is important to choose something that works for you; something that you feel both comfortable enough and satisfied enough with. Once you have picked something, try it for long enough to feel if it is having the effect you want. I recommend at least seven consecutive days.

I have been doing some version or another of The Miracle Morning for over 500 days, and I continue because I have experienced three major benefits:

1. I feel more awake and focused during the day, no matter whether I feelthat I slept enough or not.
2. I have an easier time going to bed a bit earlier at night, which is a hugewin for me as a night owl!
3. I am reading a 100-page monthly magazine that I find very interesting.

Activity #1: Take some time now to craft a morning routine that you would like to try.

Then try it. Then try it again. Try it seven days in a row to give yourself time to see how it is working for you.

Evening routines

Once again, it is important to identify what your needs are. Depending on whether you have trouble falling asleep or staying asleep, or you have trouble stopping with the day's activities to go to sleep, the recommendations won't be the same.

The purpose of an evening routine is obviously to put yourself in the best possible conditions for having a peaceful night of sleep. If you are a parent, you probably have experienced creating nighttime routines with your child(ren), whether it is a bath before bed, telling a story, listening to some music, or some other combination.

Let's start with the decision to go to bed. Some people can just pick up and go to bed in a few minutes whenever they feel tired in the evening. I used to be married to such a person. It always bewildered me.

Personally, I need time to transition, check that everything is alright, feed the cat, and prepare a few things for the next morning. And then I have my bathroom routine, cleaning my face, applying my night cream, etc. The whole thing can take up to an hour. You might be somewhere in the middle.

Whatever your style and rhythm in the evening, it is crucial to know how much sleep is enough for you and plan your evening routine accordingly. Say you get up at 7:00 and need 8 hours of sleep; you then need to turn off your light at 11:00 PM and therefore need to stop what you are doing in the evening with enough time to complete your routine before bed.

This may seem super trivial to you, and it does to me too. Except this is my single biggest tripping point in life. If you are a morning person, you might be thinking I am defective or something. If you are a night person, you can probably relate to this.

Night owls wake up in the evening and the urge to go to sleep just doesn't come, so it takes real intention, and oftentimes it goes against the energy of the moment. It may not feel like bedtime at the appointed hour needed to feel rested.

So, the night people will have an extra challenge compared with the morning people, and a nighttime routine may serve a purpose there. Here are a few ingredients of a nighttime routine; you should feel free to add your own:

- Have a soothing herbal tea, such as chamomile
- Light some candles
- Play some soft music
- Write down three things that went well for you today
- Write down one to three goals for tomorrow
- Take some time to read in bed if it helps you find sleep Take some time to journal

Activity #2: Take some time now to craft a nighttime routine that you would like to try.

Then try it. Then try it again. As I keep telling you, I recommend that you give yourself a full seven days before deciding if you like it or not!

Sleeping habits

Sleep is essential for your best possible self to have a chance of showing up. As I presented in Chapter 6, not getting enough sleep has all sorts of consequences, not the least of which is being in denial about how sleepdeprivation is affecting you. I recommend two activities for this topic. The first is a diagnostic.

Activity #3:

1. Go to bed 30 minutes earlier tonight than you usually do.
2. Don't change your alarm.
3. Notice if you wake up before your alarm.
    a. If you do, you have found your night length.
    b. If not, go to bed 30 more minutes earlier tomorrow night.
    c. Repeat until you wake up before your alarm.
4. Take stock of your sleep needs.

From this first activity, you will have a better idea of how much sleep your body requires for optimal functioning. You might try this several days in a row as there are, of course, days when you are more tired than other days.

The second activity is a stress-reducing one. Stress can mess with your sleep like nothing else! One way to relax, in general and for sleeping in particular, is to find your diaphragm. The Greeks call it the center of all expression. It is the key to how you regulate your system.

You already found your diaphragm in Chapter 7. If you need a reminder, put your thumb ½ inch to an inch below your real or imaginary bra-strap. That is your diaphragm. Now press lightly down with your thumb. As you breathe in, push your thumb away with your in-breath, and as you breathe out, your thumb should come back down.

Activity #4: Take three or four slow full breaths, in and out, as I just described. The diaphragm goes around so if you put your hands on your rib cage, you can feel the ribcage open as you breathe in and close as you breathe out.

What difference do *you* feel after doing this? Make a note of how it has affected you. It is a very easy, very portable, very accessible tool for stressreduction, which may help you find your sleep.

CHAPTER 12

Exercise

Before starting on any new exercise routine, I strongly recommend that you see a doctor. It is probably ok, however, for everyone to walk more.

The next set of practices concern exercising. Again, there are some formal practices and some informal practices. Since I have been working out in a gym with a professional coach, for about an hour, three times a week, most weeks, for almost 23 years, I have learned a few things about exercise.

I have a fairly high level workout regimen for a non-professional. and I can tell you that getting my body to work, and to work hard sometimes, has yielded diverse benefits in terms of emotion regulation, quality of sleep, and physical abilities in my day-to-day life; thus, I view exercise as the cornerstone of my equilibrium.

What can exercise do for you? You will not know that until you try!

For exercise, just like for meditation, in order to get the most benefit, it is necessary to have a regular formal practice. How you do that and what you start with depends on your current exercise level.

If you have trouble motivating yourself to exercise, it is amazing how much easier that becomes if you find someone to do it with you. The accountability to another person is a very strong motivator.

If you are completely sedentary, you could start with walking for five minutes three times a week. After you do that for a few weeks, you can increase to 10 and then 15 minutes three times a week.

Or you might sign up for and go to a yoga class. You may have noticed that signing up for the class, just like reading this book, has no impact if you don't get into action. So find someone who has a similar goal and put on your walking shoes!

If you are already somewhat physically active, and you want to increase your level of fitness because it is good for your health, the possibilities are endless. Find something that you enjoy doing; it makes it more likely that you will follow through. Which activity will work for you will depend to a large extent on your ability to self-motivate.

You may join a gym and either attend classes or get a trainer who will take your specific goals into account and build a program for and with you. There are also a number of video-based programs available on the internet. Some programs use weights, some programs use bodyweight. There are two things to check for any program you are considering starting:

1. Is the advice you are getting sound? In other words can the source of theadvice be trusted?
2. Are you motivated enough that you will follow through?

If you have answered YES to both these questions, you are good to go!

If the advice is not sound, find better advice. There is no shortage of offerings of exercise-related activities. If you do not feel motivated enough to follow through, then I send you back to Part I of the book to work on your mindset.

Let me remind you that exercising, among other things, will help you to have more willpower for other goals. This may be a sufficient motivator for some.

I may have a somewhat unusual ability to self-motivate, but I can tell you that I don't ever ask myself if I feel like working out. I schedule it, and I go when it is time to go. That became automatic after I really became aware of the benefits I was getting from my workouts.

For health reasons and for sustaining your willpower, it is desirable to have a formal exercise practice. Such a practice can be complemented, however, by more informal exercises. This is the exercise that you get in your day to day life.

Today, the World Health Organization (WHO), the US Centers for Disease Control and Prevention, the US Surgeon General, the American Heart Association, the US Department of Health & Human Services, and the National Heart Foundation of Australia all recommend that individuals take 10,000 steps a day to improve their health and reduce the risk of disease. Yup, that's right, ten thousand.

This will not happen without putting some intention behind it. You could park far away in the parking lot every time you park, and/or walk or bike instead of driving short distances. Another biggie is using the stairs. There are several reasons to use the stairs. Elevators actually use a lot of electricity to go up and down all day. So by using the stairs, you will get beneficial exercise AND save energy.

Exercise is beneficial for your health. You already know that. If you are currently not exercising or not exercising enough, you may need more than just me telling you to go exercise. In Chapter 19, you will learn five tips for forming new habits. In this chapter, I have laid out for you some known aspects of exercise and discussed my relationship to those aspects. As I do throughout this book, I urge you to figure out if and why you might want to modify your relationship to exercise, and then find an exercise routine that works for your preferences, for your schedule, and for your current body.

Activity #5: Decide on two plans of action that will improve your relationship to exercise.

Examples are:

1. Find a buddy and schedule three walks next week with them.
2. Sign-up for a gym and make an appointment with the trainer there.
3. Decide to walk for five or ten minutes at lunch time and put a reminderon your phone.

What are your plans of action? Decide this right now and then write in Table 1 when you will take your chosen actions.

CHAPTER 13

Food

I Include this chapter on food because of the impact of healthy eating on willpower, our precious ally for reaching our goals. So in this chapter, you will find my recommendations for healthy eating, which I gathered during my own quest from sources I trust. Some of those sources are in the Sources of Inspiration section at the end of the book.

A common issue with food choices is motivation. A lot of people know better and yet consume a diet full of nasty stuff. If you recognize yourself in this description, you probably need to spend some time thinking about *WHY* you might want to eat a healthier diet.

Is it so that you are better able to keep up with your kids? Is it so you can have a better time with your partner? Is it to enhance your willpower? Would it enable you do your job better? What is *your* 'WHY' for wanting to be healthier?

If this is your stumbling block, I recommend that you grab your activity booklet or a pen and a paper and take ten minutes right now to clarify that. Start writing: "I want to get healthier because…" and see what comes next.

Perhaps, you find that you lack willpower. If that is the case, I can tell you again that sleeping enough, eating well, and exercising are key supporters of willpower!

So I recommend you concentrate on those activities that benefit you and strengthen your willpower as a byproduct.

Eat organic produce as much as possible

This recommendation has two possible objections: availability of organic produce, and their price. Only you know where you stand regarding these objections.

In the case of financial issues, I would argue that by eating healthy foods, you may need to eat less of it for good nutrition and the benefit of this may offset the initial cost.

If you are interested in buying more organic produce, you might be interested in the following two lists. Dr Weil and the Environmental Working Group have identified the produce with the highest and lowest pesticide residue.

The first list, the Dirty Dozen Plus (2017), contains the produce with the <u>highest pesticide residue</u>; thus, it is most important that you buy the organic versions of these items.

- Strawberries
- Spinach
- Nectarines
- Apples
- Peaches
- Pears
- Cherries
- Celery
- Grapes
- Tomatoes
- Sweet bell peppers
- Cherry tomatoes
- Potatoes
- Cucumbers
- Lettuce

By contrast, the Clean 15 list is comprised of the following fruits and vegetables, which have the <u>lowest pesticide residue</u>. You can buy these from conventional sources with less pesticide impact on your health.

- Sweet corn
- Avocados
- Pineapples
- Cabbage
- Onions
- Sweet peas (frozen)
- Papayas
- Asparagus
- Mangoes
- Eggplant
- Honeydew melon
- Kiwi
- Cantaloupe
- Cauliflower
- Grapefruit

Pesticides in your food can be detrimental to your health so it is preferable to avoid foods with high pesticide content. For foods with lower pesticide residue, it is still possible that large amounts of pesticides and herbicides are used on the farms from which these originate, contaminating groundwater, promoting erosion, and otherwise damaging local eco-systems.

So reducing the demand for chemical-heavy foods is a contribution to your health and beyond. To help promote the health of the planet as well as your own health, it's best to buy organic whenever you can.

<u>Activity #6:</u> Decide which foods you want to start buying organic.

Reduce sugar!

For health, environmental, and willpower reasons, it is recommended to massively reduce the sugar in your diet. I discussed this in Chapter 6 but in my honest opinion, it can bear to be repeated.

Sugar has recently been promoted to the rank of #1 enemy of our health. The list of diseases that become more likely as a result of consuming too much sugar is too depressing to include here. So if you are going to make only one change in your life to improve your quality of life, this would be my pick: reduce your sugar intake. Here are some suggestions.

a) Quit sugary drinks!

Nothing is quite as bad as drinking your sugar. First off, your body doesn't count the calories you drink so drinking sugar is a sure way to take in too many calories. Having sugar water in your mouth is also bad for your teeth. On top of that, consuming that much sugar in the first place is a really bad health choice.

Start replacing all your sugary drinks with water or unsweetened herbal teas. If you cannot wean yourself off of the sweet taste, it seems that Stevia and raw honey are some of the best? better options. Artificial sweeteners, while not as bad for your teeth, are not innocuous in your blood sugar regulation mechanism, according to medical sources and also Isabel de Los Rios, the founder of the Beyond Diet program. So still be careful of artificial sweeteners.

b) Quit industrial wheat-based products.

Industrial cakes, white bread and pasta, cookies, candy etc. may include added sugar, but they also turn into sugar in your bloodstream very quickly. So-called whole wheat produced industrially is not much better, in terms of glycemic index. If you like bread, I recommend that you either make your own or find some that is made using artisanal methods with good quality ingredients.

c) Reduce hidden sugars.

A more advanced activity is to reduce your hidden sugar consumption. For this, you must look at the labels of the food you eat. A good rule of thumb is that if it ends in –ose, it is probably sugar, as in Sucrose, Maltose, and Dextrose, among others. Anything with syrup in the name is also likely to be a form of sugar.

One way to reduce hidden sugars is to eat natural foods.

<u>Activity #7:</u> Identify one to three sugar-related habits that you will change, for better health and willpower.

Adjust your meat consumption

Red meat has received a lot of negative attention for its environmental and health impact and also for the sometimes downright disgusting ways it is produced.

Back in 2008, the documentary *Food, Inc.* depicted some of the most shocking shenanigans of the food industry, concerning red meat among other practices. The alarming evidence on the negative health impacts of red meat is mitigated by other studies, but regardless, the idea of eating bleached hamburgers remains disgusting to me.

If you want to cut out meat altogether, it is important that you research what vitamins and minerals you will need to supplement.

My personal take on the issue is to eat less meat and to eat only high quality meat if you do eat it. I eat only free-range locally grown chickens and pasture-raised beef; I seldom eat pork.

I urge you to question your position on meat. What next step are you willing to take?

<u>Activity #8:</u> Do you wish to change your meat consumption? Take some time to ponder this. If you do, how will you do it?

Seasonings

When I describe some of my food choices, people often wonder about taste, as though eating less meat and more vegetables is synonymous with eating a bland diet. Not at all!

There are a myriad of seasonings. Pepper, ginger, turmeric, parsley, coriander, and mint, just to name a few, add flavor and health benefits for some. You can also add brewer's yeast for B vitamins and minerals.

The possibilities are endless. If you are looking for healthy yummy recipes, I recommend www.beyonddiet.com, which I have already mentioned. Check it out and be assured that I am not getting a commission.

CHAPTER 14

Practices for a Positive Mindset

I recommend five practices for a positive mindset. They are Breathing into the Present Moment, Gratitude, Self-Compassion, Forgiveness, and Visualization – the Hindsight Window.

Breathing into the present moment

The first and most essential pillar for improving your mindset is to cultivate the ability to be present in the moment. The most direct and fool-proof way to do that is to spend some time every day focusing on your breath.

Start small, one minute when you wake up, and one minute before going to sleep. Increase gradually, see what you prefer. Maybe doing it in the morning gives you a better start to your day, and maybe doing it right before bed helps you settle for a good night's sleep.

If you have a long commute during which you are not driving, that might be a perfect time to develop a centering practice.

Practice this in the way that is most comfortable for you to fit into your daily routine, but practice it daily and you will see results.

Activity #9: Schedule one-minute of focused breathing twice a day for seven days, and then do it! At the end of seven days, note how you like it.

Gratitude

The practice of gratitude has so many benefits that it is considered a metastrategy for cultivating happiness and well-being. Having a practice of cultivating presence in the moment will help you get in touch with those things that bring positivity into your life and will facilitate the feeling of gratitude.

To incorporate the gratitude activity into your routine, I recommend that you start by doing it once a week, maybe Sunday evening. To practice gratitude, take some time to quietly reflect on the week that has elapsed. Let one to three pleasant things come to your mind. Write a short description of each event.

It really is more powerful to write it down rather than just think it; studies have shown that unequivocally. So you might want to get yourself a gratitude journal and have one page per week.

If you find that you enjoy it a lot, you can of course do it more often, but you want to avoid a situation in which it becomes an obligation and you start feeling like you have trouble coming up with three things to write about.

Emergency gratitude can be found in the realization that you have access to this present moment. If you are really stuck and cannot find a single thing to write about, I suggest the following:

> "I am grateful for the present moment, for in it lies the possibility of the future I am creating."

— Sonia Weyers

Gratitude, or gratefulness also comes in handy when you want to get out of "negative," unpleasant emotions. If you can muster the discipline to connect to something you feel grateful for in your life, you will find that your "negative" emotion is gone.

Activity #10: Next time you feel that an unpleasant emotion has a strong hold on you, look for something in your life you feel really grateful for and bring up the feeling of gratefulness.

Activity #11: Schedule 15 minutes in the next week to write about three things you are grateful for from the previous week. Be very specific in your descriptions and feel gratefulness blossom in your chest.

Forgiveness

Holding a grudge is a sure way to lower your sense of well-being. Perhaps you will have a sense of self-righteousness, but I don't think that will make you happy. Yet, forgiving can be difficult.

This activity is for you if you are feeling wronged in some way and you are having trouble letting go. It is based on the work of Fred Luskin from Stanford University.

Activity #12:

Start by thinking of a situation in which you feel wronged, you feel like someone has done you some harm that you are not able to forgive, to let go of. There are 9 steps.

1. The first step is to become intimately familiar with how you feel aboutwhat happened. Do you feel sad? Do you feel angry? Do you think it was unfair?

    Try to clarify the way in which you feel wronged and the emotional impact it is having on you. Then you can tell a few trusted people about your experience.

2. Make a commitment to yourself to feel better. Remember that forgiveness is for you, to free yourself of these unpleasant feelings you are harboring.

3. Realize that forgiveness does not necessarily imply reconciliation with people who offended you nor does it mean condoning their actions; rather, your aim is to blame the offenders less and take their offenses less personally.

4. Become aware of what is happening: you are distressed over the hurt feelings and thoughts you are having at this time. You are not actually hurting from what happened then.

5. When the upset feelings are too much, it is important to soothe yourself. You can do the diaphragm exercise, do some deep breathing, and/or go into nature, whatever works best for you.

6. If you do not have the power to make something happen, it is best to give up expecting it. You might have been demanding something from the person who hurt you that they were not willing or able to give you. This causes suffering.

   Remind yourself that you can hope for and work hard for what you want, but you may not have the power to make it happen.

7. Focus on finding a way to get your positive goals met other than through the experience that has hurt you.

8. Realize that a life well-lived is your best revenge. If you focus on your wounded feelings, you give power to the person who has caused you pain. Instead of that, look for the beautiful things around you such as love, beauty and kindness.

   Put your energy into appreciating what you have rather than focusing on what you do not have.

9. Include your heroic choice to forgive in the way you look at your past.

When you have successfully forgiven someone who had hurt you, you will understand why it is so important. The weight lifted off your shoulders will help you enjoy life more and create more pleasant memories.

Self-compassion

This activity is a good one to pull out when you face a difficult situation. If you are used to beating yourself up when you don't measure up to your expectations, it may be difficult so start small. Maybe once a week is enough to start with.

This activity is composed of the three parts of self-compassion:

1. mindfulness
2. common humanity
3. self-kindness

In a moment when you are feeling difficult emotions, you may be tempted to tell yourself that you shouldn't be feeling this way. This is probably the most common, yet unproductive way to respond to a difficult emotion. Try picking a statement that reflects how you feel and say it to yourself: "This is a moment of suffering" or "this is hard" or "this hurts."

This is a way to mindfully connect with your emotional experience in the moment without judging it as either good or bad. The next step is to recognize an element of common humanity. Remind yourself of this common humanity by saying, "Suffering is part of life," or "Everyone struggles in their life."

The third and last step is to put your hands over your heart and try saying, "May I be kind to myself." In this way, you express self-kindness. Variations on the statement can include "May I give myself the support that I need" or "May I be strong in this moment."

Activity #13: Choose a phrase for each part of self-compassion: mindfulness, common humanity, and self-kindness. Use it next time you are falling short of your expectation. Notice how that feels.

A second self-compassion practice is the Metta meditation that you will find in Chapter 17 on spiritual practices.

Visualization – The Hindsight Window

The last activity for emotional health is visualization. The common way to visualize is to center yourself and then muse about the best possible outcome for some aspect of your life.

The visualization I propose to you for this activity is a bit different, and it is one of the most powerful techniques I have come across. Eric Edmeades talks about it beautifully: it is about shortening the Hindsight Window. Let me explain what this is.

You probably have somewhere in your memory, an event that was difficult, perhaps even downright tragic, and then, later in your life, a moment when you realized some good things happened as a result.

I can certainly credit my struggles in life for giving me the skills I have today for enhancing my life. Had I had a happier start in life, I would never have embarked on this quest, which is so satisfying today.

The hindsight window is the time between the difficult event and the time at which you can see the secondary benefit you have derived from that difficult event. It seems clear, from this perspective, that the shorter your hindsight window the happier you will be. Conversely, the longer your hindsight window the less happy you will be.

Activity #14:

1. Pick an event or situation that you are currently struggling with. 2. Ask yourself, "Why might I be grateful for this one day?"
3. Ask yourself again, "Why might I be grateful for this one day?"
4. Ask yourself yet again, "Why might I be grateful for this one day?"
5. When you begin to find answers to this question, you will have a newperspective on what is happening to you, and you will see that it will be

OK.

So, in the words of Eric Edmeades, "The more gratitude you can have for your past, the more faith you can have for your future!"

Shrinking your hindsight window is a powerful way to get more happiness in your life and more gratitude for your past.

CHAPTER 15

Self-Care Practices

For this chapter, I want you to start by reflecting on what makes you feel good in your life or what else you think would make you feel good. You are looking for concrete time-bound actions such as taking a warm bath, going for a walk outside, or curling up in bed with a good book.

These are practices that you can do for yourself, by yourself. This is not to say you will suddenly become self-sufficient and not need anyone else. It is, however, a useful skill to be able to soothe and nurture yourself.

<u>Activity #15:</u> Find five self-care activities that appeal to you. Schedule them. Find an accountability partner and let them know what you are doing.

Let's detail each part of this activity.

Can you come up with five activities that will make you feel better if you do them? If you have trouble coming up with five, see if you can take inspiration from the following list.

- Take a warm bath
- Go for a run
- Go for a leisurely stroll in nature
- Sit in a comfortable chair and sip a warm beverage

- Read a book that interests you
- Listen to music you like
- Sit outside in the sun
- Light some candles and diffuse lavender essential oil in your bedroom and rest
- Whatever you can think of that will make you feel good without jeopardizing your future happiness

Do you have your five self-care actions? Now, I want you to take your calendar and schedule them all, with a minimum of one a week.

When you have done that, I want you to contact someone whom you feel comfortable talking to about the steps you are taking to improve your life. Tell them what you have scheduled and ask them if they would be willing to hold you accountable.

In addition, you may want to write your activities in your activity booklet or in Table 1 from the appendix.

I will do:

1.

2.

3.

4.

5.

On: (date and time)

1.

2.

3.

4.

5.

Great! Now you have some self-care activities scheduled and accountability put into place. Feel free to expand on this chapter and keep adding new selfcare activities to your weekly schedule.

CHAPTER 16

Social Life

There are two activities in this chapter. The first one is an activity for seeing people. The second one is planning and executing acts of kindness.

For the first activity, you will organize and plan outings to see people. There are a couple of simple steps to do this. First, I propose that you consider three broad categories of people to see: friends, family, and social groups.

Friends and family speak for themselves and by "social groups," I mean any collective setting you may be part of. Maybe you attend an exercise class, maybe you are part of a walking group, or maybe you sing in a choir.

Second, I invite you now to select one member of each category: one friend, one relative or group of relatives, and one specific social group. If you do not have a collective setting at this time, I invite you to think of one that you would like to try.

Third, for each of these people or settings, select a time and place and activity that you will schedule. You may want to coordinate with them, of course, and when you have done that, record your plan in your activity booklet.

As a result of this activity, you will have scheduled three separate events. I am counting on you to now mark those on your calendar and actually follow through. The other part of the activity is then to mindfully enjoy these events that you have scheduled and after you complete each one, reflect how it has improved your experience and take notes in Table 1 and your activity booklet or notebook.

<u>Activity #16</u>: Schedule one activity with one member of each of the three categories: Friends, Family, and Social groups.

<u>Friends:</u>
   Who?_____

   Where?_____

   What?_____

   When?_____

<u>Family:</u>

Who?_____

Where?_____

What?_____

When?_____

Social group:

Who?_____

Where?_____

What?_____

When?_____

My hope for you is that once you have taken action on each of these plans, you will have a better sense of how your social life impacts your experience of life.

The next activity is very simple and very effective; it is to do something generous. There are several studies backing up the idea that generosity breeds happiness. I suggest that you try it out!

Activity #17: Schedule a generous act, do it and feel the impact.

CHAPTER 17

Spiritual Practices

In this chapter, I suggest four spiritual practices that are not linked to religious activity. If you practice a religion, you may already have your spiritual practices as part of that, but even so, you may be interested in trying these: Meditation, Connecting with Nature, Loving Kindness Meditation, and Visualization.

Meditation

There are several approaches to meditation. The one I am most familiar with is the type learned in Mindfulness Based Stress Reduction (MBSR) programs. As I discussed at length earlier in this book, the practice of mindfulness involves focusing one's attention on something, oftentimes the breath or physical sensations, without judgment.

In the last ten years, mindfulness has gone from being an esoteric practice for the select few to being in every self-help publication, online or offline; it appears in every health and well-being recommendation; it has even entered into the business world with its touted benefits on productivity.

It seems only a slight exaggeration to say that the ambient message is: to practice mindfulness assures you a great life and to not practice it... well do it at your own risk. I find it difficult to position myself in relation to such binary messages, and yet, I can truthfully say that taking the flagship 8-week MBSR class has had a profound impact on my life.

I just mentioned the MBSR curriculum, but what seems to me to be essential for finding the key to our empowered life is to have some sort of contemplative practice; a practice that quiets down our mind so that a more intuitive, wise, and deep part of ourselves can better be heard.

There are many types of contemplative practices, and if you either have experience with such a practice or feel attracted to another practice, I strongly encourage you to follow your heart. I found mindfulness, and it is working for me. I urge you to find something that works for you.

An MBSR teacher and practitioner, Dave Potter, has a website on which he offers the MBSR training for free. Doing it on the internet is, of course, not the same as doing it in a live group, but it can be a good way to get a flavor of the practice.

Whatever the practice you choose, there are two basic ways to practice. One is the formal practice and the other is the informal practice. A formal practice would be to sit quietly for some amount of time, every day, at similar times: for example, you could do it as part of your morning or evening routine. You can sit and focus on your breath, you can do a body scan, or you can listen to guided meditations. The common aspect of all these is that you devote time to the practice.

And then there is the informal part of the practice, which can be both a consequence and a reinforcing aspect of the formal practice. This can be called mindful living.

When you are stuck in traffic and you start getting annoyed, you might catch yourself, take a mindful breath, and then become more aware of your reaction. When you are doing dishes or standing in line, you might take the opportunity to scan your body for unnecessary tensions or become aware of unproductive thoughts that are racing through your mind. When you go tuck your child in at the end of a long exhausting and stressful day, you might think to center yourself first by taking three deeps breaths, for example.

The informal practice is the flower that blooms from the previous season's growth of the formal practice. It is not likely that you will be able to shift your attitudes in the flow of your daily life if you don't make some personal investment in some formal practice first.

<u>Activity #18</u>: Experiment with a formal contemplative practice.

Pick a formal practice that works for you. I recommend that you make this a part of either your morning or your evening routine. At the moment, I start my morning routine with my formal practice of breath meditation, affirmations, and visualization for 8 to 12 minutes.

All these small ways of becoming more present throughout your day will have, I promise you, a positive impact on your experience of your life and on your relationships.

Connecting with Nature

The second spiritual activity is "Connecting with Nature." What I mean by this is to have an experience with nature. This can be as simple as gardening, watering your flower pots or planting something in one. It can also be as grand as contemplating mountains, the sea, the woods, large rural areas, or the sky, and feeling that you are connected to something bigger than yourself.

For maximum effect, I encourage you to find some nature, to breathe it in, and to think about how it all came about, how it happened that you can look at this scene. It may take some practice, but my hope for you is that you begin to have an experience of being one with nature, and the feeling of inner peace that comes with that.

<u>Activity #19</u>: Breathe in some nature and reflect on how it all came about. Notice how you feel.

Visualization

The third practice I suggest to you is a Visualization. You can lie down in a comfortable position, close your eyes, and begin to visualize a world compatible with your spiritual values. You may want to visualize a world in peace, a world of tolerance, a world of respect, and just let your mind show you what that would look like to you.

If you prefer to write, you can set a timer and write for 15 minutes, describing this world in as much detail as possible.

Activity #20: Set aside 15 minutes, make yourself comfortable in a quiet place, and visualize your ideal world. Notice how you feel afterwards.

This is an opportunity to live, in your imagination, in the world such as you wish for it to be. Our reptilian brains don't differentiate between imagination and reality, so you can give yourself an experience of living in your ideal world through your imagination.

Enjoy your voyage!

Loving Kindness Meditation

The fourth and last spiritual practice I suggest is a Loving Kindness Meditation, also called Metta. In this meditation, you repeat specific words and phrases that evoke a boundless warmhearted feeling.

To practice this, find a peaceful place and sit in a comfortable and relaxed position. You may want to start by taking a couple of deep breaths. You will start by directing the well-wishes towards yourself. As you say the phrases, allow yourself to feel the intentions they express.

Activity #21: Practice the Metta meditation described here.

May I be safe and protected,

May I be happy and peaceful,

May I be healthy and strong,

May I live with ease, and

May I be held, in loving kindness

After directing the loving-kindness to yourself, bring to mind someone whom you feel warmly towards and direct the well-wishes to them. It may be easier if you bring up an image of them in your mind's eye.

May you be safe and protected,

May you be happy and peaceful,

May you be healthy and strong,

May you live with ease, and

May you be held, in loving kindness.

As you continue with this meditation, you will direct the well-wishes to other people.

Next you will direct them to someone you feel neutral towards, maybe someone you barely know.

After that, direct them to someone you have difficulty with.

When you send loving-kindness to someone you have difficulty with, you may experience some opposite feelings such as anger, grief, or sadness. Don't worry about this and try not to judge yourself for having these feelings. See if you can observe those feelings and continue the meditation anyway.

If it is too difficult, maybe try with someone whom you have less difficulty with. The practice is aimed to cultivate feelings of loving-kindness in your own heart and, with practice, you can then wish good things upon even those who have harmed you in some way.

You end the meditation by sending loving kindness to all living beings:

May we be safe and protected,

May we be happy and peaceful,

May we be healthy and strong,

May we live with ease, and

May we be held, in loving kindness.

This is one of my favorite meditations! How do YOU like it? I encourage you to take some notes in your activity booklet or your notebook to capture your feelings and reflections.

CHAPTER 18

Your New Goals and Habits

> "We are what we repeatedly do. Excellence, then, is not an act but a habit."
>
> – Aristotle

Congratulations, you have considered 21 activities that can improve your happiness levels. This chapter presents the last two activities to lead you to build a master plan with specific healthy habits that can drive your happiness.

It is time to look through your notes and decide on the new habits you want to incorporate into your life. Looking back to the four areas of focus, Your Physical Health (Chapter 6), Your Emotional Health (Chapter 7), Relationships (Chapter 8) and Spirituality and Meaning (Chapter 9), I invite you to choose 1 goal for each area. For example, for your emotional health, goals could be:

- I want to feel less stressedor
- I want to be less reactiveor
- I want to feel more positive emotions

Take time now to prioritize one goal for each of the four areas of focus. You can write down your goals in your activity booklet. If you feel completely satisfied with one of the areas, you can leave that area blank, but I encourage you to wonder if things couldn't be even better.

Activity #22: Define your priority goals.

For my physical health, my top goal is:

For my emotional health, my top goal is:

For my relationships, my top goal is:

Regarding spirituality and meaning, my top goal is:

You should now have anywhere between 0 (not so likely given that you have read this book to this point) and 4 goals you are interested in pursuing. Next, you will choose some actions that will move you closer to your goals.

But first, let us go over some considerations about getting into routines and creating habits.

Getting into routines

Part I of this book on mindset and attitude showed you how to best ensure that you will follow through with the actions YOU decide to take. To further help you implement the needed changes, you should take note of how actions become habits.

A lot of claims have been made about how long it takes to create a habit. Twenty-one days has been thrown around a lot. Yet, the latest research from University College London, says it takes 66 days on average to make a new behavior habitual. The truth is that it really depends on people and activities. Here are things that can help you succeed in creating new habits.

1. If you have identified WHY you want to change a habit or create a new one, and if that WHY is sufficiently important to you, you will have a much easier time drumming up motivation. *I want to do this because I*

read an article that said it was a good idea is unlikely to provide much of any motivation. ***I want to do this because it will improve my quality of life for the long run*** is much more likely to work. So <u>pick habits that you can justify to yourself</u>.

2. Tie the new habit to an existing habit. Christine Carter discusses thistactic in her free webinars on creating habits that stick.

   For example, if your goal is to floss more, but you already brush your teeth, then you would do well to piggy back your new flossing habit to your pre-existing teeth brushing habit.

   When you pick a new activity that you wish to start, see if you can identify an activity you already do and make your new objective to add the new behavior to the existing habit.

3. Defensive pessimism. Think about the various ways in which you couldget derailed and plan how you will get back on track. You can go back to Chapter 2 if you need a reminder of the detailed steps for defensive pessimism.

4. Get a buddy. It helps a lot to have someone who will help you on thepath to accountability, and you might be able to return the favor by helping them to change some of their behaviors and improve their life.

5. Circle back to motivation. If you feel that summoning the neededmotivation is your biggest challenge, I encourage you to start with one behavioral change at first and know that you can always go back to Part I for your shot of motivation.

Creating healthy habits has one wonderful benefit: you won't need so much willpower that way; your habits will just kick in!

<u>Activity #23:</u> Create your Action Plan.

Using your notes from your activity booklet or your notebook and from Table 1, ask yourself the following two questions for each activity:

1. Did this activity make me feel more peace, meaning or joy?

2. How can this activity contribute to my goals?

Let the answers to these two questions guide you to select up to three activities per goal. You can write down your plan in your activity booklet, in your notebook or you could type it up and frame it somewhere prominent, whatever you think makes it most likely that you will follow through with it.

GOAL I:
– Action 1:
– Action 2:
– Action 3:

GOAL II:
– Action 1:
– Action 2:
– Action 3:

GOAL III:
– Action 1:
– Action 2:
– Action 3:

GOAL IV:
– Action 1:
– Action 2:– Action 3:

This ends the "Getting into Action" part. I hope you were able to find activities that resonate with you and that you will follow through on the plan you have just created.

If you haven't already, I encourage you to join our Facebook Group "Happiness Now! A Guided Journey."

Conclusion

Congratulations, you have reached the end of this book. I hope you feel motivated to bring change into your life. Before I send you off to the next greater version of you, let's sum up what you have learned.

In Part I, you learned the ingredients of motivation. In Part II, you discovered important areas of focus: Your Physical Health, Your Emotional Health, Your Relationships, Your Spirituality and Meaning. In Part III, you chose among 23 different activities those you want to incorporate into your life starting RIGHT NOW!

It is only through action that you will really discover and change. In this book, I have given you the very best information and actions to take your experience of life to the next level.

More broadly, I encourage you to seek new experiences as much as you can. It is through experience that you learn holistically, through body, mind, and soul.

On your way to a better life, remember to use the following set of questions to stay true to yourself. They will help you to seek experiences that are meaningful for you.

- Where? Where are you starting from, what are your beliefs about your situation? Are these beliefs serving you or can you improve on them?
- What? What are you trying to achieve, have you visualized your desired outcome? Be clear and specific about your vision.
- Why? What is your purpose in trying to achieve this? Your purpose is what drives you and this is probably the most important thing to consider.
- How? And finally, how are you going to go about achieving this goal, what are the steps, what is your strategy?

I hope you have found some answers in this book and that you have indeed found greater peace, meaning and joy. I wish you all the best in your search for a better life!

Writing this book was a new experience for me, and I learned a tremendous amount about myself in the process. I would not have written it without a reader like you in mind. Please stay in touch in the Facebook group "Happiness Now! A Guided Journey." Thank you!

Printed in Great Britain
by Amazon